More! Low Carb Recipes Fast & Easy

by
Belinda Schweinhart

with
Chaddie Letson

Brass Pig, LLC

The information in this book is based upon the latest data made available by government agencies, food manufacturers and trade associations. The data contained herein is the most complete and accurate information available as this book goes to press. It is important to note that all nutrient breakdowns for processed foods are subject to change by, and are different between, manufacturers without notice and therefore may vary from printing to printing.

ISBN 0-9671821-1-5

Copyright © 2001 by Brass Pig, LLC

All rights reserved. No part of this publication may be reproduced, stored in a retrieval system, or transmitted, in any form or by any means, electronic, mechanical, photocopying, recording, or otherwise without the prior written permission of the copyright owner.

Printed in the United States of America

First Printing   January, 2001

Published by

Brass Pig, LLC
PO Box 43091
Louisville, KY 40253
1-888-229-9677
www.LowCarbRecipes.com

www.LowCarbCookbooks.com

Introduction

This book contains real, great tasting, easy recipes. They are all low carb, no sugar, no flour recipes suitable for anyone following the Atkins diet, the Protein Power Plan, the Carbohydrate Addicts Diet, the Zone and the Neanderthin diet as well as those needing no sugar recipes for diabetic diets. When was the last time you ate a really good cookie without feeling guilty? Try the almond cookie on page 130.

I know there are hundreds, if not thousands, of low carb recipes on the Internet. I've personally tried many of them. The problem I've found is that 1) they don't taste very good and I'm not wasting any of my carbs on something that is marginal, 2) the carb counts frequently aren't right and 3) they are too complicated.

(Note – All carb counts used in this cookbook have been obtained from the USDA Internet data base. See page 12 for address.)

I owned and operated a restaurant for six years to a daily packed house crowd and am well aware of pleasing the customer, repeatability and ease of a recipe, the need to be specific with ingredient brands and just plain eye appeal. I spent a lot of time doing up front developing on a recipe so it could be prepared by <u>anyone</u> from the instructions on the wall.

My best advise for anyone wanting to follow a low carb diet is to get the book of the plan you are going to follow and read the book – all of it. There are a lot of self-proclaimed experts due to their experiences, but nothing can replace getting the facts from the real experts. Again, read the books.

Check our companion web site for all the latest low carb books and cookbooks at **www.LowCarbCookbooks.com**.

Belinda Schweinhart

Table of Contents

Resources 6-22
        What can I buy at the grocery? ...health food store? ...on the Internet?
        Where to find carb counts for other foods not listed
        Carb counts for spices
        Carb counts for assorted flours
        Sugar substitute equivalents chart
        Helpful measurements

FAQs 23-26
        Blanching Almonds – how do I do it?
        Do sugar substitutes have carbs?
        Fearn® soya powder - is it the same as soy flour?
        not/Starch® - how do I use it?
        Nut Flour - how do I make it?
        Oat Flour - how do I make it?
        Splenda®- what is it?
        Steaming Cauliflower – how do I do it?
        Why are brand names listed in some recipes?
        Can I use Stevia as a sugar substitute?
        Xanthan gum - what is it?
        Can soy flour be substituted for Atkins® baking mix?

Appetizers and Snacks 27-36

Drinks 37-42

Breads 43-52

Soups and Sauces 53-62

Breakfast Dishes 63-72

Salads 73-82

Vegetables 83-98

Entrees 99-126

Desserts 127-152

Index 153-156

About the Authors...

Belinda Schweinhart started the Atkins diet in January, 1998, after trying every other diet available. None worked, at least not for very long. She knew diabetes and low blood sugar were prevalent in her family. After 6 months, she had lost 40 pounds, and more importantly, gone from size XXL to size MEDIUM! Cholesterol went from 251 (with HDL of 54 – test didn't show other numbers, darn it!), to 234 (with HDL of 61, LDL of 140 and tryglycerides of 165) after only six months, and had cholesterol of 225 (with HDL of 64, LDL of 126 and tryglycerides of 174) after one year. *After two years of following the low carb diet, her cholesterol is now only 184 (with HDL of 65, LDL of 96 and triglycerides of 114).* Her tests are better with every test.

It has been 36 months and she has continued to keep the weight off and still feels great eating low carb!

Chaddie Letson found her way to the low carb way of thinking because of her husband's onset of adult diabetes. Her husband's doctor suggested that he consider the low carb diet. After 3 months on the diet, he lost 40 pounds, lowered his bad cholesterol (LDL) by 30 points and increased his good cholesterol (HDL) by 20 points. But the most remarkable result was that he was able to go off his diabetes medicine . . . his blood sugar went from 356 to 146!

We love this way of eating! We can no longer call this a "diet."

RESOURCES

What can I buy at the grocery?

Five Brothers® Alfredo or Alfredo Mushroom Sauce
2 grams carbs per ¼ cup (0 g fiber)

Five Brothers® Tomato Alfredo Sauce
7 grams carbs per ¼ cup (1 gram fiber)

Ragu® Double Cheddar or 4 Cheese Alfredo or Light Parmesan Alfredo Pasta Sauce
2 grams carbs per ¼ cup (0 g fiber)

Ragu® Roasted Garlic Parmesan or Classic Alfredo Pasta Sauce
3 grams carbs per ¼ cup (0 g fiber)

Healthy Choice® Mushroom Alfredo or 4 Cheese Alfredo Sauce
3 grams carbs per ¼ cup (0 g fiber)

Newman's Own® Pasta Sauce – several flavors
9 grams carbs per ½ cup (3 grams fiber)

Breakstone's® Sour Cream
1 gram carbs per 2 TBSP. (0 g fiber)

Frigo® Cheese Heads String Cheese
less than 1 gram carbs per piece (0 g fiber)

Kraft® Deluxe American Cheese Slices *(not cheese food)*
less than 1 gram carbs per slice (0 g fiber)

Parmesan Cheese – grated
.2 grams carbs per 1 TBSP. (0 g fiber)

Kraft® Shredded Parmesan Cheese
1 gram carbs per 1/3 cup (0 fiber)

Frigo® Ricotta Cheese, skim
2 grams carbs per ¼ cup (0 g fiber)

Cottage Cheese, 4% small curd only
2 grams carbs per ½ cup (0 g fiber)

RESOURCES

Kraft® Philadelphia Cream Cheese
.8 grams carbs per 1 ounce (6.4 grams per 8 ounces)

Half & Half (cream)
.6 grams carbs per 1 TBSP. (10.4 grams per cup)

Heavy Whipping Cream
.4 grams carbs per 1 TBSP. (6.6 grams per cup)

Reddi Wip® Whipped Light Cream *(contains sugar)*
less than 1 gram carbs per 2 TBSP.

Healthy Life® 100% Whole Wheat Bread
16 grams carbs per 2 slices (6 grams fiber)

Healthy Life® White Bread
16 grams carbs per 2 slices (4 grams fiber)

Irene's Health Bakery® Garlic Gluten Bread
4 grams carbs per slice (0 fiber)

Irene's Health Bakery® German Rye Bread
5 grams carbs (1 gram fiber)

Jell-O® Instant Sugar-Free Pudding Mix *(contains aspertame)*
6 grams carbs per ¼ package mix
(8 grams carbs per ¼ package for chocolate mix)

Jell-O® Sugar-Free Gelatin Mix *(contains aspertame)*
1 gram carbs per ¼ package

Hillshire Farm® Beef Smoked Sausage
8 grams carbs per 1-pound package

Swanson® Fat-Free Chicken Broth
1 gram carbs per cup

Lunchmeats, Hotdogs, etc (not Light or Fat-Free)
Various – read the labels!

Canned Chicken
0 grams carbs per ¼ cup

RESOURCES

Canned Tuna
    0 grams carbs per ¼ cup (0 g fiber)

Pork Rinds
    0 grams carbs (0 g fiber)

Rudolph's® Bacon Snaps Microwave Pork Rinds
    0 grams carbs (0 g fiber)

Bacon Bits, real
    0 grams carbs (0 g fiber)

Eggs, large
    .6 grams carbs each (0 g fiber)

Pour-A-Quiche® Three Cheese and Broccoli & Cheddar
    4 grams carbs per 1/6 pie (1 gram and .5 grams fiber)

Pour-A-Quiche® Spinach & Onion
    7 grams carbs per 1/6 pie (.5 grams fiber)

Hellmann's® Real Mayonnaise
    0 grams carbs (0 g fiber)

Salad Dressings (not Lite or Fat-Free)
    Various - read the labels!

Assorted Extracts
    1.4 grams carbs per 1 TBSP. (0 g fiber)

Assorted Spices
    Various - see page 16

Walnut pieces chopped
    16.5 grams carbs per cup (8.0 grams fiber)

Pecan pieces chopped
    16.5 grams carbs per cup (11.4 grams fiber)

Macadamia Nuts
    18.4 grams carbs per cup (12.5 grams fiber)

Pumpkin Seed Kernels
    30.5 g carbs per cup (8.9 g fiber)

RESOURCES

Almonds
  28.0 g carbs per cup (16.7 g fiber)

Hazelnuts
  19.2 g carbs per cup (7.3 g fiber)

Peanuts, oil roasted
  27.3 g carbs (13.3 g fiber)

Peanuts, dry roasted
  31.0 g carbs (11.5 g fiber)

Macadamia Nuts
  17.2 g carbs (10.7 g fiber)

Planters® Dry Roasted Sunflower Kernels
  6 grams carbs per ¼ cup (4 grams fiber)

Fifty 50® Peanut Butter (no sugar added)
  6 grams carbs per 2 TBSP. (2 grams fiber)

Swiss Miss® Diet Hot Cocoa Mix
  4 grams carbs per envelope

Worcestershire Sauce
  1 gram carbs per 1 tsp.

Kikkoman® Soy Sauce
  0 grams carbs

ReaLemon® Lemon Juice
  0 grams carbs per 1 tsp.

Sugar Twin® (or Brown), Splenda® or Equal® Granular Sweetener
  1 gram carbs per 2 tsp.

Sugar Twin®, Sweet 'n Low®, Equal® or Splenda® Packet Sweetener
  1 gram carbs per packet

Splenda® Tablets Sweetener
  1 gram carbs per tablet

RESOURCES

Splenda® Liquid Sweetener
0 carbs (0 fiber)

Saco® Unsweetened Cocoa
2.6 grams carbs per 1 TBSP. (1.3 grams fiber)

Hershey's® Unsweetened Cocoa
3.0 grams carbs per 1 TBSP. (1 gram fiber)

Nestlé® Unsweetened Cocoa
3.0 grams carbs per 1 TBSP. (2 grams fiber)

Baker's® Unsweetened Baking Chocolate
8 grams carbs per 1 ounce (4 grams fiber)

Nestlé® Unsweetened Baking Chocolate
10 grams carbs per 1 ounce (6 grams fiber)

Good Humor® Sugar Free Popsicle *(sweetened with aspartame)*
3 grams carbs each

Good Humor® No Sugar Added Creamsicle *(sweetened with aspartame)*
5 grams carbs each

Kool-Aid® or Wylers® unsweetened drink mix
0 g carbs (0 g fiber)

Kool-Aid® or Wylers® or Tang® sugar-free drink mix *(sweetened with aspartame)*
0 g carbs (0 g fiber)

Crystal Light® sugar-free drink mix *(sweetened with aspartame and acesulfame potassium)*
0 g carbs (0 g fiber)

Veryfine® Fruit2O flavored water *(sweetened with Splenda)*
0 g carbs (0 g fiber)

Diet Ice Botanicals® flavored water *(sweetened with Splenda)*
0 g carbs (0 g fiber)

What can I buy at the health food store?

Hodgson Mill® Vital Wheat Gluten
    32 grams carbs per cup (16 grams fiber)

Bob's Red Mill® Vital Wheat Gluten Flour
    6 grams carbs per 1/4 cup (0 grams fiber)

Xanthan Gum
    8 grams carbs per 1 TBSP. (9 grams fiber)

Guar Gum
    6 grams carbs per 1 TBSP. (6 grams fiber)

Fearn® Soya Powder
    7 grams carbs per ¼ cup (3.5 grams fiber)

Unsweetened Coconut
    2 grams carbs per 3 TBSP. (1 grams fiber)

Arrowhead Mills® Peanut Butter *(no sugar added)*
    6 grams carbs per 2 TBSP. (1 gram fiber)

GNC® Soy Baking Mix
    5 grams carbs per ¼ cup (1 gram fiber)

Designer Protein® Mix *(Strawberry, Chocolate and Vanilla Praline)*
    2.5 grams carbs per 1 level scoop (less than 1 gram fiber)

NOW® Stevia Packets *(herbal sugar substitute)*
    1 gram carbs per packet

Bran-a-crisp® crackers
    6 grams carbs (6 grams fiber)

Bob's Red Mill® Oat Flour
    18 grams carbs per 1/3 cup (2 grams fiber)

Arrowhead Mills® Oat Flour
    20 g carbs per 1/3 cup (4 g fiber)

RESOURCES

Wasa Crispbread Fiber Rye
  7 grams carbs each (2 grams fiber)

Soy Flour
  9 grams carbs (6 grams fiber)

Flax Seed Meal
  4 grams carbs (4 grams fiber)

Westbrae® Natural West Soy Unsweetened Soy Beverage
  5 grams carbs per 1 cup (4 grams fiber)

Sweet-n-Safe® Sweetener *(contains acesulfame potassium)*
  1 gram carbs per packet (= 4 teaspoons sugar equivalency)

Pumpkorn®
  4 grams carbs (2 grams fiber) per 1/3 cup

Just The Cheese®
  2 grams carbs (0 fiber) per bag

Kavli® Crispy Thin Crispbread
  13 grams carbs (2 grams fiber) per 3 pieces

Yves® Veggie Pizza Pepperoni
  4 grmas carbs (3 grams fiber) per 16 slices

CARB COUNTS For OTHER foods not listed :

http://www.nal.usda.gov/fnic/cgi-bin/nut_search.pl
(USDA for foods in general)

http://www.cyberdiet.com/ni/htdocs/sc_ffquest.html
(for fast foods)

http://www.stanford.edu/group/ketodiet/ketomeds.html
(for medicines)

<u>The Complete Book of Food Counts</u> by Corinne T. Netzer (Dell Publishing, 1997)

<u>Carbohydrates Calories & Fat in your food</u> by Dr. Art Ulene (Avery Publishing Group, 1995)

Carb counts for Assorted Flours:

Almond Meal	18.8 carbs (11.2 fiber) / cup
Cashew Meal	44.8 carbs (4.1 fiber) / cup
Oatmeal	51.8 carbs (8.8 g fiber) / cup
Oat Flour	60.0 carbs (12.0 g fiber) / cup
Full Fat Soy Flour	29.9 carbs (8.2 g fiber) / cup
Defatted Soy Flour	38.4 carbs (17.5 g fiber) / cup
Walnut Meal	11.0 carbs (5.4 g fiber) / cup
Wheat Bran	38.8 carbs (25.7 g fiber) / cup
Wheat Germ	51.8 carbs (13.2 g fiber) / cup
Rye Flour	79.0 carbs (14.9 g fiber) / cup
Rice Bran	41.2 carbs (17.4 g fiber) / cup
Pecan Meal	63.4 carbs (13.6 fiber) / cup
Low Fat Peanut Flour	18.8 carbs (9.5 fiber) / cup
Macadamia Meal	18.4 carbs (11.2 fiber) / cup
Hazelnut Meal	12.5 carbs (7.3 fiber) / cup
Whole Wheat Flour	76 carbs (3 g fiber) / cup
All-Purpose Flour	85 carbs (0 fiber) / cup
Fearn® Soya Powder	28 carbs (14 g fiber) / cup
GNC® Soy Mix	20 carbs (4 g fiber) / cup
Vital Wheat Gluten	32 carbs (16 g fiber) / cup (Hodgens Mill®)
Wheat Gluten Flour	24 carbs (0 fiber) / cup (Bob's Red Mill®)

1 cup wheat flour = 3/4 cup soy flour
1/2 cup nut meal
1-1/3 cup oat flour
1-1/4 cup rye flour
2/3 cup GNC® Soy mix
1 cup Fearn® soya powder

2 cups wheat flour = 1-1/4 cup vital wheat gluten flour
+ 3/4 cup oat flour
+ 1/4 cup soy flour

RESOURCES

CARB COUNTS for SPICES

1 TBSP. — USDA Nutrient Values

ALLSPICE, GROUND	4.327 g carbs (1.296 g fiber)
ANISE SEED	3.351 g carbs (0.978 g fiber)
BASIL, GROUND	2.743 g carbs (0.796 g fiber)
BAY LEAF, CRUMBLED	1.349 g carbs (0.473 g fiber)
CARAWAY SEED	3.343 g carbs (2.546 g fiber)
CARDAMOM, GROUND	3.971 g carbs (1.624 g fiber)
CELERY SEED	2.688 g carbs (0.767 g fiber)
CHERVIL, DRIED	0.933 g carbs (0.215 g fiber)
CHILI POWDER	4.099 g carbs (2.565 g fiber)
CINNAMON	5.430 g carbs (3.692 g fiber)
CLOVES, GROUND	4.040 g carbs (2.257 g fiber)
CORIANDER LEAF, DRIED	0.935 g carbs (0.187 g fiber)
CORIANDER SEED	2.749 g carbs (2.095 g fiber)
CUMIN SEED	2.654 g carbs (0.630 g fiber)
CURRY POWDER	3.663 g carbs (2.092 g fiber)
DILL SEED	3.641 g carbs (1.393 g fiber)
DILL WEED, DRIED	1.730 g carbs (0.422 g fiber)
FENNEL SEED	3.033 g carbs (2.308 g fiber)
FENUGREEK SEED	6.477 g carbs (2.731 g fiber)
GARLIC POWDER	6.108 g carbs (0.160 g fiber)
GINGER, GROUND	3.822 g carbs (0.675 g fiber)
MACE, GROUND	2.677 g carbs (1.071 g fiber)
MARJORAM, DRIED	1.029 g carbs (0.308 g fiber)
MUSTARD SEED, YELLOW	3.913 g carbs (0.739 g fiber)
NUTMEG, GROUND	3.450 g carbs (1.456 g fiber)
ONION POWDER	5.243 g carbs (0.371 g fiber)
OREGANO, GROUND	2.899 g carbs (0.675 g fiber)
PAPRIKA	3.846 g carbs (1.422 g fiber)
PARSLEY, DRIED	0.672 g carbs (0.134 g fiber)
PEPPER, BLACK	4.148 g carbs (1.696 g fiber)
PEPPER, RED OR CAYENNE	3.001 g carbs (1.325 g fiber)
PEPPER, WHITE	4.871 g carbs (1.860 g fiber)

RESOURCES
15

POPPY SEED	2.085 g carbs (2.570 g fiber)
POULTRY SEASONING	2.427 g carbs (0.418 g fiber)
PUMPKIN PIE SPICE	3.880 g carbs (0.829 g fiber)
ROSEMARY, DRIED	2.114 g carbs (1.406 g fiber)
SAFFRON	1.373 g carbs (0.082 g fiber)
SAGE, GROUND	1.215 g carbs (0.360 g fiber)
SAVORY, GROUND	3.024 g carbs (2.011 g fiber)
TARRAGON, GROUND	2.411 g carbs (0.355 g fiber)
THYME, GROUND	2.749 g carbs (0.800 g fiber)
TURMERIC, GROUND	4.415 g carbs (1.435 g fiber)

<u>OTHER</u>

BAKING POWDER	3.822 g carbs (0.027 g fiber)
BAKING SODA	0 g carbs (0 g fiber)
CREAM OF TARTAR	5.535 g carbs (0.018 g fiber)

RESOURCES

Where do I buy on the Internet?

Atkins Nutritionals
185 Oser Ave.
Hauppauge, NY 11788
800-6-ATKINS
888-7-ATKINS fax
www.atkinscenter.com
www.atkinsdiet.com
•Atkins foods, nutritionals

(The) Baker's Catalog
PO Box 876
Norwich, VT 05055-0876
1-800-827-6836
1-800-343-3002 fax
www.kingarthurflour.com
•flours, dough conditioners appliances

Carber's Choice Company
1751 Mulbery Road
Cherry Tree, PA 15724
www.carberschoice.com
•assorted foods, appliances, house brands

CarbSmart
PO Box 608
Lake Forest, CA 92630
877-279-7091
949-829-9524 fax
www.carbsmart.com
•assorted foods, books, house brands and nutritionals

Diet Depot
10422 Taft Street
Pembroke Pines, FL 33026
877-260-8361
954-432-2977 fax
www.dietdepot.com
•Asst. foods, nutritionals, books

D'Lites of Shadowood
9975 Glades Road
Boca Raton, FL 33434
888-937-5262
561-488-4203 fax
www.lowcarb.com
•Asst. foods, nutritionals, books

Platinum Nut
PO Box 325
Hughsun, CA 95326
209-883-1707
209-883-4554 fax
www.eatalmonds.com
•almonds and almond flour

Expert Foods
PO Box 1855
Ellicott City, MD 21041
www.ExpertFoods.com
•not/Sugar, not/Starch, not/Cereal, Mousse mix, frozen fudge bar mix, other mixes

RESOURCES
17

Global Drugs, Inc.
6448 Old Banff Coach Rd. SW
Calgary, Alberta Canada T3H2H4
403-246-1227
403-246-1228 fax
www.globaldrugs.com/pharmacy/fsearch.htm
• Asst. sugar substitutes

GNC (General Nutrition Center)
In your neighborhood shopping center
800-477-4462 (store locator)
www.gnc.com
• GNC Soy Baking Mix, asst. bars, Designer Protein, asst. drink mixes, nutritionals

Ketogenics, Inc.
1330-13 Lincoln Ave.
Holbrook, NY 11741
800-943-5386
631-580-2817 fax
www.ketogenics.com
• house brand bread, muffin, syrup mixes

La Tortilla Factory
3635 Standish Ave.
Santa Rosa, CA 95407
www.latortillafactory.com
• low carb tortillas

Lewis Brothers Bakeries, Inc.
P.O Box 6471
500 N. Fulton Ave.
Evansville, IN 47710
(812) 425-4642
• Healthy Life Breads

Life Services Supplements, Inc.
3535 Hwy 66 Bldg. #2
Neptune, NJ 07753
800-542-3230
732-922-5329 fax
www.lifeservices.com
• Asst. house brand foods, drinks, mixes, nutritionals

Lindora, Inc.
3505 Cadillac Ave. Suite N2
Costa Mesa, CA 92626
800-LINDORA
714-668-9341 fax
www.leanforlife.com
• house brand soup mixes, drink mixes

Low Carb Connoisseur
Enrich Enterprises, Inc.
1208 N. Main St.
Anderson, NC 29621
864-224-0245
864-419-9631
www.low-carb.com
• Asst. foods, nutritionals, candies

Low Carb Dieter's Page
PO Box 92
Winter Park, FL 32790
407-644-5981 fax
www.lowcarbdieters.com
• Asst. foods, books, unique products

RESOURCES

Low Carb Living Market
1465 Encinitas Blvd. Suite H
Encinitas, CA 92024
760-634-5316
760-753-6315 fax
www.lowcarbliving.com
• Asst. foods

Low Carb Nexus
116 E. main St. Suite E
Jamestown, NC 27272
336-812-8845
336-812-8847 fax
www.lowcabnexus.com
• Asst. foods, nutritionals and house brand foods

McNeil Specialty Products Inc.
New Brunswick, NJ
800-SPLENDA
www.splenda.com
• Splenda granular and packets

Morico Health Products
2102 Kotter Ave.
Evansville, IN 47715
800-524-4473
812-485-0006 fax
www.morico.com/locarb.html
• House brand ice cream, baking, drink, bread mixes

Netrition
20 Petra Lane
Albany, NY 12205
888-817-2411
518-456-9673 fax
www.netrition.com
• Asst. foods, nutritionals

Nuts4U
PO Box 1864
Sugar Land. TX 77487
800-nuts4u2
www.nuts4u.com
• Asst. nuts and nut flours

Stevita Stevia Co., Inc.
7650 US Hwy. 287 #100
Arlington, TX 76001
888-STEVITA
www.stevitastevia.htm
• Stevita brand stevia

Sugar Free Paridise
18747 W. Dixie Hwy.
N. Miami Beach, FL 33180
800-991-7888
305-682-8222 fax
www.sugarfreeparadise.com
• Asst. foods and house brands

SynergyDiet
234 N. Allen Ave.
Pasadena, CA 91106
877-877-1558
626-229-0624 fax
www.synergydiet.com
www.zerocarb.com
• Asst. foods, candies

(The) Vitamin Shoppe
4700 Westside Ave.
North Bergen, NJ 07047
800-223-1216
800-852-7153 fax
www.vitaminshoppe.com
• Atkins bars, drinks, nutritionals

RESOURCES

MORE...

www.lowcarbchocolates.com

www.lowcarboliscious.com

www.naturesflavors.com

www.optimumnutr.com

www.lowcarboutfitters.com

www.lowcarbcenter.com

www.traderjoes.com

www.lowcarbgrocery.com

www.steelsgourmet.com

www.fiberrich.bigstep.com

RESOURCES

Helpful measurements:

3 teaspoons = 1 tablespoon

2 tablespoons = 1 ounce

12 teaspoons = 4 tablespoons = 1/4 cup

24 teaspoons = 8 tablespoons = 1/2 cup

48 teaspoons = 16 tablespoons = 1 cup

5-1/3 tablespoons = 1/3 cup

1 cup = 1/2 pint = 8 ounces

2 cups = 1 pint = 16 ounces

4 cups = 2 pints = 1 quart = 32 ounces

8 cups = 2 quarts = 1/2 gallon = 64 ounces

16 cups = 4 quarts = 1 gallon = 128 ounces

---

8 drops = 1/8 teaspoon
16 drops = 1/4 teaspoon
32 drops = 1/2 teaspoon
64 drops = 1 teaspoon
192 drops = 1 tablespoon
384 drops = 1/8 cup (2 tablespoons)

---

1 quart casserole = 9" pie plate = 8" round pan = 7½ x 3½ x 2½ " loaf pan = 6" soufflé dish

1½ quart casserole = 10" pie plate = 9" round pan = 8½ x 3½ x 2½" loaf pan = 7" soufflé dish

2 quart casserole = 8 x 8 x 2" pan = 11 x 7 x 1½" pan = 9 x 5 x 3"loaf pan = 8" soufflé dish

2½ quart casserole = 9 x 9 x 2" pan = 11¾ x 7½ x 1¼" pan
3 quart casserole = 8 x 8 x 3½" pan = 13½ x 8½ x 2" glass dish

Sugar Substitute Equivalencies

Sugar	Splenda®, Sweet 'n Low®, Equal® Packets	Splenda®, Sugar Twin®, Equal® Granular/Brown	Splenda® Tablets	Sweet 'n Low® Liquid *check other brands	Splenda® Liquid	Stevia Packets	Stevita® Liquid *check other brands	Stevia Powder-Liquid U-Mix See page 26
1 teaspoon	1/2	1 tsp.	1	10 drops	3 drops	1/2	1/6 tsp.	4 drops
1 tablespoon	1-1/2	1 TBSP.	3	30 drops	9 drops	1-1/2	1/2 tsp.	12 drops
1/4 cup	6	1/4 cup	12	1-1/2 tsp.	1/2 tsp. + 4 drops	6	2 tsp.	3/4 tsp.
1/3 cup	8	1/3 cup	16	2 tsp.	3/4 tsp.	8	2-2/3 tsp.	1 tsp.
1/2 cup	12	1/2 cup	24	1 TBSP.	1 tsp. + 8 drops	12	4 tsp.	1-1/2 tsp.
2/3 cup	16	2/3 cup	32	4 tsp.	1-1/2 tsp.	16	5-1/3 tsp.	2 tsp.
3/4 cup	18	3/4 cup	36	4-1/2 tsp.	1-1/2 tsp. + 12 drops	18	6 tsp.	2-1/4 tsp.
1 cup	24	1 cup	48	2 TBSP.	2-1/4 tsp.	24	8 tsp.	1 TBSP.

Notes

Frequently Asked Questions

- Blanching Almonds – how do I do it?
- Do sugar substitutes have carbs?
- Fearn® soya powder - is it the same as soy flour?
- not/Starch® - how do I use it?
- Nut Flour - how do I make it?
- Oat Flour - how do I make it?
- Splenda®- what is it?
- Steaming Cauliflower – how do I do it?
- Why are brand names listed in some recipes?
- Can I use Stevia as a sugar substitute?
- Xanthan gum - what is it?
- Can soy flour be substituted for Atkins® Baking mix?

FAQs

Blanching Almonds – how do I do it?

Drop almonds into a pan of boiling water and cook for 30-45 seconds. Remove and drain. Cool with cold water. To remove almond skins, squeeze each between fingers. Dry by placing on cookie sheet and baking at 375° for 2-3 minutes. Cool before grinding. (Almonds do not have to be blanched before grinding. This is a personal preference.)

Do sugar substitutes have carbs?

Yes. However, the carbs come from the fillers being used in the particular substitute form. Granular form has more carbs than packets. Packets have more carbs than tablets. And liquid form has the fewest carbs, and sometimes zero. Check the labels. (Sugar substitutes always taste better when two different types are used together instead of a single source.)

Fearn® soya powder - is it the same as soy flour?

No. Soy flour is made by grinding whole dry soybeans into flour in the same way wheat kernels are ground into flour. It often contains considerable hull material, is more coarse, and may even be raw. Soy flour is often dry-toasted after grinding to improve the flavor and digestibility. Soya powder is made by cooking the soybeans before grinding. It is finer than soy flour and usually has a better flavor.

not/Starch® - how do I use it?

1 teaspoon of not/Starch® is equal to 1 teaspoon of cornstarch. However, if more than 1 teaspoon of cornstarch is to be substituted, start with ONLY 1 teaspoon of not/Starch® and sprinkle in more as needed. It does not need heat to thicken, just time. If recipe has thickened too much, add additional liquid to thin. (Unfortunately, this product can only be purchased on the Internet – manufacturer's web site is www.ExpertFoods.com.)

Nut Flour - how do I make it?

Place nuts in blender, food processor or coffee grinder. (Use only small amounts at a time.) Grind until flour or meal consistency. You may want to sift out the larger pieces to either discard or re-grind.

Oat Flour - how do I make it?

Place regular oatmeal (not instant) in blender, food processor or coffee grinder. (Use only small amounts at a time.) Grind until flour or meal consistency. You may want to sift out the larger pieces to either discard or re-grind.

Splenda®- what is it?

It comes in granular, packet, tablet and liquid forms. Each form has different carb counts. Be sure to check the package or see page 21. (Sugar substitutes always taste better when two different types are used together instead of a single source.)

Steaming Cauliflower – how do I do it?

Place head or flowerettes in 1-1/2 quart microwaveable dish. Add 1/2 cup water and cover. Microwave for 5 minutes on high. Turn or stir pieces. Recover and microwave additional 5 minutes. Check for tenderness and adjust time as necessary for your microwave.

Why are brand names listed in some recipes?

Not all brands of the same food item have the same carb counts, fiber counts or taste. If a particular brand has the best combination of these three attributes, I will name it.

FAQs

Can I use Stevia as a sugar substitute?

Yes. White stevia powder is the easiest to work with. However, the pure powder is 200 to 300 times the sweetness of sugar. For a more usable form, mix 2 tsp. White stevia powder with 2 TBSP. warmed water. Stir until dissolved and store in the refrigerator. See chart on page 21 for usage. (Sugar substitutes always taste better when two different types are used together instead of a single source.)

Xanthan gum - what is it?

Xanthan gum is used to help non-gluten flours rise. It can also be used to give a smooth, creamy texture to sauces. It has a unique ability to hold particles of food together, making it a good stabilizer.

not/Sugar® - what is it?

not/Sugar® is a vegetable fiber substance used to replace the bulk and mouthfeel of sugar. Sugar substitutes have no volume and contribute nothing to the texture. It does not change the taste in any way. Recipes in this book can be made without this ingredient without effecting the taste. (Unfortunately, this product can only be purchased on the Internet – manufacturer's web site is www.ExpertFoods.com.)

Can soy flour be substituted for Atkins® Baking mix?

No. Soy flour is simply soy flour. Atkins® Baking Mix is a mix of soy flour and leavening agents to help it rise. (Think of the difference between wheat flour and Bisquick® Baking Mix.) GNC® Soy Baking Mix can be substituted for the Atkins® brand and doesn't have the soy taste.

Appetizers and Snacks

Black Bean Dip
Cheese Crackers
Cheese Spread
Cinnamon Crunchies
Crab & Spinach Spread
Dried Beef Roll-ups
Horseradish Mold
Pepperoni Bites
Meatball Bites
Popsicles
Scallion Bean Pancakes
Shrimp Dip
Spinach-Garlic Spread

Fast & Easy Tips

- Macadamia nuts are the easiest snacks.

- Pumpkorn® and Just Cheese® are prepackaged and easy to pack. Check your local health food store.

- Always keep pork rinds on hand for the munchies – in several different flavors. Try different brands, not all taste porky. Try the microwave brands.

- Cheese balls are easy and low in carbs. Serve with pork rinds, Wasa Crisps® or celery sticks.

- Nuts are fast and easy for snacks, but watch the carb counts.

- Keep precooked meats in the fridge for easy protein snacks.

Black Bean Dip
Serves 12

1	clove	garlic -- chopped
2		jalapeno chile pepper -- seeded and chopped
15	ounces	Eden® black soybeans -- rinsed and drained
14	ounces	artichoke hearts -- rinsed and drained
3	ounces	cream cheese -- softened
2	tablespoons	lemon juice
1	tablespoon	parsley -- chopped
1/2	teaspoon	salt

In food processor or blender, combine all ingredients and blend until smooth.

Per serving: 7.0 g carbohydrates   78.0 calories
                3.8 g fiber   4.2 g fat
                                        4.9 g protein

Cheese Crackers
Serves 4

1/2	pound	cheddar cheese -- shredded

Place small mounds of shredded cheese (approximately 1 tablespoon) on to microwavable dish lined with parchment paper. Cheese should be spread to 1/4" or less. Microwave for 1 minute on high to start. Continue to microwave in 10-20 second increments until bubbly. When crisp enough, note this time for future use.

Per serving: 0.7 g carbohydrates   228.5 calories
                0 g fiber   18.8 g fat
                                        14.1 g protein

Variations: Other cheeses can also be used: Swiss, Havarti, Parmesan, American, etc.

APPETIZERS and SNACKS

Cheese Spread
Serves 8

1	cup	sour cream
1	cup	cheddar cheese -- shredded
1		green onion -- minced
2	tablespoons	parsley -- chopped
1/2	teaspoon	dried thyme
1/2	teaspoon	dried rosemary
1/2	teaspoon	pepper

In medium mixing bowl, combine all ingredients and mix well. Cover and chill before serving.

Per serving: 3.4 g carbohydrates   127.9 calories
              0.6 g fiber   10.8 g fat
                                     5.0 g protein

Cinnamon Crunchies
Serves 4

3	ounces	pork rinds -- plain
4	tablespoons	butter -- melted
12	packets	sugar substitute — see page 21
1	tablespoon	cinnamon

Break pork rinds into smaller pieces. Place into zip-lock bag. Drizzle melted butter over pork rinds and shake to coat evenly. In separate bowl, combine sugar substitute and cinnamon. Slowly add mixture to zip-lock bag and continue to shake. Place on cookie sheet.

Bake at 250° for 8-10 to crisp.

Per serving: 4.4 g carbohydrates   238.3 calories
              0.9 g fiber   19.0 g fat
                                     13.9 g protein

APPETIZERS and SNACKS

Crab & Spinach Spread
Serves 15

2	packages	frozen chopped spinach -- cooked and drained
1	cup	butter
1/2	cup	onion -- chopped
1-1/2	cups	Parmesan cheese -- grated
12	ounces	crab meat -- canned

Press excess water from cooked spinach with paper towels. In medium saucepan, melt butter. Add onion and sauté until translucent. Add spinach, Parmesan cheese and crab. Mix well. Serve warm.

Per serving: 2.0 g carbohydrates   176.0 calories
               1.2 g fiber   14.9 g fat
                                            9.3 g protein

Dried Beef Roll-ups
Serves 2

8	ounces	cream cheese -- softened
2	tablespoons	onion -- chopped
14	slices	Armour® dried beef

In small bowl, mix cream cheese and onion. Spread mixture evenly on dried beef slices. Roll up and serve chilled or at room temperature.

Per serving: 5.5 g carbohydrates   460.7 calories
               0.1 g fiber   41.0 g fat
                                            16.3 g protein

APPETIZERS and SNACKS

Horseradish Mold
Serves 12

1	envelope	Knox® unflavored gelatin
4	tablespoons	water — cold
1	cup	water
1	package	sugar-free gelatin mix -- small, lemon
5	ounces	horseradish
1	cup	Hellman's® mayonnaise
1	cup	sour cream

Dissolve gelatin in cold water. In separate container, boil cup of water in microwave. Dissolve lemon gelatin in hot water. Blend both mixtures together. Let cool. Add in horseradish, mayonnaise and sour cream. Pour into greased mold. Chill until firm.

Per serving: 2.3 g carbohydrates   190.6 calories
              0.2 g fiber   18.7 g fat
                                      3.1 g protein

Pepperoni Bites
Serves 48

8	ounces	cream cheese -- softened
1	cup	Mozzarella cheese -- shredded
1	cup	Parmesan cheese -- grated
5	ounces	water chestnuts -- diced
10	ounces	frozen spinach -- chopped
48		pepperoni slices

In medium bowl, combine cream cheese, cheeses, water chestnuts and well drained spinach. Place pepperoni slices on cookie sheet. Place about a teaspoonful of filling on each slice.

Bake at 350° for 20 minutes.

Per serving: 1.2 g carbohydrates   62.8 calories
              0.3 g fiber   5.2 g fat
                                      2.9 g protein

APPETIZERS and SNACKS

Meatball Bites
Serves 4

1/2	pound	ground beef
1/4	cup	water
2	teaspoons	instant minced onion
		salt -- to taste
		pepper -- to taste
		Spike® seasoning -- to taste
4	slices	bacon

In medium mixing bowl, combine ground beef, water and seasonings. Mix well. Shape into 8 balls. Cut bacon strips in half crosswise. Wrap bacon around a meatball and secure with toothpick. Place all meatballs in skillet and cook, turning frequently, until bacon is crisp and beef is done.

If adding sauce, be sure to add carb counts.

Per serving: 0.0 g carbohydrates   212.4 calories
               0.0 g fiber   18.2 g fat
                                          11.4 g protein

Popsicles
Serves 8

1	package	sugar-free gelatin mix -- small
1	package	sugar-free drink mix
1/2	cup	sugar substitute - see page 21
1	cup	boiling water
2	cups	cold water

Add gelatin mix, drink mix and sugar substitute to the boiling water. Stir to dissolve. Add cold water and mix well. Pour into popsicle mold or ice cube trays.

Per serving: 2.0 g carbohydrates   11.0 calories
               0 g fiber   0 g fat
                                          0.5 g protein

Scallion Bean Pancakes
Serves 8

4	slices	bacon
3	cups	Eden® black soybeans -- rinsed and drained
1	teaspoon	white wine vinegar
2		egg yolks
4		green onions -- sliced thin
1	teaspoon	white wine vinegar
4	tablespoons	butter -- melted
2	tablespoons	parsley -- minced
1	teaspoon	dry mustard
2	tablespoons	soy sauce

In a skillet, cook bacon until crisp and brown. Remove bacon and place on paper towels. Leave drippings in skillet. Place soybeans, vinegar and egg yolks in blender or food processor. Blend until pureed. (Use a small amount at a time if necessary.) Pour mixture into a separate bowl. Add crumbled, cooked bacon and chopped green onions. Mix well.

Reheat the bacon drippings in the skillet. Drop bean batter by the tablespoonfuls into the skillet. Fry for 2-3 minutes per side. Keep cooked pancakes warm in a 200° oven until ready to serve.

In a separate bowl, whisk together remaining ingredients. Drizzle over pancakes and serve warm.

Note: Pancakes can be made ahead and re-fried a second time just before serving. This makes them a little crisper too.

Per serving: 12.3 g carbohydrates   202.0 calories
              7.3 g fiber   13.3 g fat
                                       11.8 g protein

APPETIZERS and SNACKS
35

Shrimp Dip
Serves 16

1	pound	shrimp, cooked -- peeled and deveined
		lemon juice
1	cup	celery -- finely chopped
1/2	cup	onion -- finely chopped
		salt -- to taste
16	ounces	cream cheese -- softened
1/4	cup	Hellman's® mayonnaise

Sprinkle all shrimp with lemon juice. Separate 1 cup of shrimp and mash well. Chop remaining shrimp into small pieces. Blend celery, onion and salt into cream cheese. Add shrimp and mix well. Chill before serving.

Per serving: 1.2 g carbohydrates   154.1 calories
               0.2 g fiber   13.0 g fat
                                            8.2 g protein

Spinach-Garlic Spread
Serves 16

10	ounces	frozen chopped spinach -- thawed
1/8	cup	half & half
1/8	cup	water
1	tablespoon	oil
2	teaspoons	garlic -- minced
1/2	teaspoon	salt
2	dashes	hot pepper sauce
11	ounces	cream cheese -- softened

Cook spinach according to package directions. Drain well and press out excess liquid. In medium pan, combine half & half, water, oil, garlic, salt and pepper sauce. Add cubed cream cheese and cook over medium heat until cheese has melted. Add spinach and mix well. Serve warm or chilled.

Per serving: 1.4 g carbohydrates   82.8 calories
               0.5 g fiber   7.9 g fat
                                            2.1 g protein

Favorite Recipes

DRINKS

Café Latte
Cappuccino
Café au Lait
Frappuccino (Frozen)
Hot Chocolate
Lemonade
Mochaccino

Fast & Easy Tips

- Coffee has become everyone's favorite drinks. The variations are limitless with sugar-free flavor syrups.

- Don't forget the multitude of flavored teas.

- Remember Tang®? It's now available sugar-free.

- Sugar-free flavored waters are now in the grocery stores.

- Sugar-free soft drinks are now available in many flavors, not just cola. And different sugar substitutes are being used. Check the labels.

DRINKS

Café Latte
Serves 1

1/3	cup	coffee, brewed -- strong
1/2	cup	half & half
1	tablespoon	sugar substitute – see page 21

An espresso or French roast would be good for this recipe. In small pan, heat half & half over low heat until warm. Whip the hot half & half in a blender for 1 minute. Pour brewed coffee into large mug. Pour half & half and sugar substitute into coffee and stir.

Variation: To make Café Mocha add 1 teaspoon sugar free chocolate extract.

Per serving: 7.0 g carbohydrates   165.3 calories
              0.0 g fiber   13.9 g fat
                                    3.7 g protein

Cappuccino
Serves 4

2-2/3	cups	coffee, brewed -- strong
1-1/3	cups	half & half
4	tablespoons	sugar substitute – see page 21

An espresso or French roast would be good for this recipe. Heat half & half over medium heat until hot. Whip the hot half & half in a blender for 1 minute. Pour hot coffee equally in 4 cups, about 1/3 full. Add sugar substitute. Pour liquid part of whipped half & half equally in cups, about another 1/3 full. Top each cup with remaining foam.

Per serving: 5.6 g carbohydrates   114.3 calories
              0.0 g fiber   9.3 g fat
                                    2.6 g protein

Variations: Add flavor extracts of your choice.

Café au Lait
Serves 4

2	cups	coffee, brewed -- strong
2	cups	half & half
4	tablespoons	sugar substitute — see page 21

An espresso or French roast would be good for this recipe. Heat half & half over medium heat until hot. (Optional: Whip the hot half & half in a blender for 1 minute.) Pour the hot coffee and hot half & half simultaneously into 4 regular sized cups. Add sugar substitute.

Per serving: 7.2 g carbohydrates   166.1 calories
               0.0 g fiber   13.9 g fat
                                         3.7 g protein

Frappuccino (Frozen)
Serves 4

1-1/2	cups	coffee
1/2	cup	half & half
1/2	cup	sugar substitute — see page 21
1/2	teaspoon	not/Sugar®
1	teaspoon	chocolate extract
1/8	teaspoon	vanilla extract
1/4	teaspoon	salt
3	cups	ice cubes -- crushed

Combine coffee, half & half, sugar substitute, not/Sugar®, extracts and salt in blender. Blend on medium speed for about 15 seconds. Add ice and blend until smooth. Pour into glasses. Top with whipped cream, if desired.

Per serving: 4.9 g carbohydrates   55.1 calories
               0.1 g fiber   3.5 g fat
                                         1.0 g protein

For caramel version: Add 2 tablespoons sugar-free caramel extract.

DRINKS
41

Hot Chocolate
Serves 1

3/4	cup	water
2	teaspoons	unsweetened cocoa powder
2	packets	sugar substitute — see page 21
	dash	salt
1/2	teaspoon	vanilla extract
4	tablespoons	whipping cream
1	teaspoon	not/Sugar®

Microwave water in large mug. Add cocoa and sugar substitute. Mix until lumps dissolve. Add remaining ingredients and mix well.

Per serving: 7.0 g carbohydrates   228.4 calories
              2.3 g fiber   22.5 g fat
                                      2.0 g protein

Lemonade
Serves 4

3-1/4	cups	water
1/2	cup	ReaLemon® lemon juice
1/2	cup	sugar substitute — see page 21

Combine water, sugar substitute and lemon juice in 1 quart pitcher. Mix well. Chill.

Per serving: 4.0 g carbohydrates   12.0 calories
              0.0 g fiber   0.0 g fat
                                      0.0 g protein

Mochaccino
Serves 4

1	cup	hot coffee -- brewed strong
1-1/2	cups	half & half
4	tablespoons	unsweetened cocoa powder
4	tablespoons	sugar substitute — see page 21
	dash	cinnamon

An espresso or French roast would be good for this recipe. In medium saucepan, mix half & half, cocoa, sugar substitute and cinnamon. Cook over medium heat, whisking constantly until mixture is hot. Pour mixture into blender. Process 30-40 seconds until frothy. Pour coffee into 4 mugs. Slowly pour mixture equally into each mug. Sprinkle with cinnamon.

Per serving: 8.6 g carbohydrates   137.8 calories
               1.8 g fiber   11.2 g fat
                                          3.8 g protein

BREADS

Basic Bread
Cheese Bread
Crepes
Cheese Taco Shells
Cinnamon Nut Bread
Cinnamon Rolls
Herbed Crackers
Wheat Germ - Cheese Bars
Herb and Cheese Muffins

Fast & Easy Tips

- Buying Healthy Life® 100% Whole Wheat Bread is by far the easiest and best solution.

- Bake the Basic Bread and freeze 2 pieces in a package.

- Try the low carb whole wheat tortillas from La Tortilla Factory® for a great bread substitute. See page 17 for details.

- Homemade bread doesn't keep as long as commercial bread. Use leftover bread for bread crumbs. Toast until hard and grind in your blender. Store in the freezer until needed.

Basic Bread
Serves 16

3/4	cup	water -- warmed
2	tablespoons	whipping cream
2	teaspoons	butter extract
3	tablespoons	oil
2		eggs
1	tablespoon	baking powder
1/2	teaspoon	salt
2	packets	sugar substitute — see page 21
1-1/3	cups	Bob's Red Mill® Vital Wheat Gluten Flour
1/3	cup	Bob's Red Mill® oat flour
1/3	cup	Fearn® Soya Powder -- sifted
1/2	cup	Hodgson Mill® Wheat Bran
2	teaspoons	xanthan gum
1	teaspoon	sugar
2	packages	rapid rise yeast for Bread Machines

Place warm water, whipping cream, extract, oil and eggs in bottom of bread machine canister. In separate bowl, mix baking powder, salt, sugar substitute, gluten flour, oat flour, soya powder, bran and xanthan gum. Stir until well blended. Pour dry mixture into bread machine canister. Make a well in the top of the dry mixture. Place the sugar and yeast in the well. Set bread machine on dough cycle only. While kneading, check dough ball. It should be smooth, not sticky or with a lot of flour still in the bottom. Add very small amounts of either gluten flour or water to get a nice dough ball.

When machine has completed one kneading cycle, remove the dough and place it in an 8x4 greased loaf pan. Spray the top of dough with oil. Place in a pre-heated (turned off) oven to rise for 45 minutes. Do not let bread rise too large, it will deflate.

Bake at 350° for 55-60 minutes. Remove from pan. Let cool completely before slicing. *(Note: The bread machine can be used to bake if it has a cycle that kneads and rises only once before baking.)*

Per serving: 6.1 g carbohydrates   98.4 calories
               1.7 g fiber   4.5 g fat
                                           9.7 g protein

Cheese Bread
Serves 16

1	recipe	Basic Bread — see page 45
1	cup	sharp cheddar cheese — shredded
3	tablespoons	fresh scallions — chopped
1	tablespoon	fresh parsley — chopped
1	tablespoon	fresh basil — chopped

Follow directions for Basic Bread and add the extra ingredients before kneading.

Per serving: 6.3 g carbohydrates   127.4 calories
              1.7 g fiber   6.8 g fat
                                       11.5 g protein

Crepes
Serves 8

2		eggs — beaten
1/3	cup	oat flour
1/4	teaspoon	salt
1/3	cup	half & half
1/3	cup	water
		oil

In medium bowl, combine all ingredients except oil. Mix until batter is smooth. Let stand for 1 hour. Heat a small skillet until hot. Coat bottom of skillet with oil. Pour rounded tablespoon of batter into heated oil. Quickly move pan so batter covers bottom of pan evenly. Cook for 1 minute or until bottom of crepe is done. Turn crepe. Cook until both sides are done. Stack finished crepes until done. (Crepes may be frozen.)

Per serving: 3.1 g carbohydrates   44.1 calories
              0.5 g fiber   2.5 g fat
                                       2.3 g protein

Variation: Dessert Crepes - substitute 2 teaspoons sugar substitute for salt.

Cheese Taco Shells
Serves 1

1/3	cup	cheddar cheese -- shredded.

Place shredded cheese on to microwavable dish lined with parchment paper. Cheese should be spread to 1/4" or less. Microwave for 1 minute on high to start. Continue to microwave in 10-20 second increments until bubbly. When crisp enough, note this time for future use. While still flexible, remove cheese while still on paper on place over a rolling pin or glass to form taco shell shape. Let cool. Remove paper when possible. Other cheeses can also be used: Swiss, Havarti, Parmesan, American, etc.

Per serving: 0.5 g carbohydrates   152.2 calories
               0.0 g fiber   12.5 g fat
                                          9.4 g protein

Variations: Taco Meat on page 125 and refried beans on page 89.

Cinnamon Nut Bread
Serves 16

1	recipe	Basic Bread -- see page 45
1/4	teaspoon	maple extract
1	teaspoon	cinnamon
1/2	cup	walnuts

Prepare bread as directed adding extract to liquid ingredients and cinnamon and walnuts to dry ingredients. Top with Icing if desired (see page 42 or 48).

Per serving: 6.3 g carbohydrates   104.4 calories
               1.8 g fiber   5.0 g fat
                                          10.0 g protein

Cinnamon Rolls
Serves 24

1		Basic Bread -- see page 45
1		egg
4	tablespoons	butter -- melted
4	teaspoons	cinnamon
1	cup	sugar substitute — see page 21

Prepare bread as directed including one additional egg. After dough has kneaded, remove from machine and divide into two equal pieces. Place piece of dough between 2 pieces of sprayed waxed paper. Roll into thin rectangle. (Dough will fight back, roll harder.) Remove top piece of waxed paper. Spread half of melted butter on dough. Sprinkle with half of cinnamon. Sprinkle with half of sugar subtitute. Starting from long side of rectangle, roll dough, leaving waxed paper out. Place roll in freezer for 15 minutes. Remove and slice into 1 inch rolls. Place rolls in greased baking pan. Spray the top of dough with oil. Place in a pre-heated (turned off) oven to rise for 30 minutes

Bake at 375° for 15 minutes. Top with Icing (see page 142 or 148).

Per serving: 5.4 g carbohydrates   90.0 calories
                1.3 g fiber   5.1 g fat
                                             6.7 g protein

Herbed Crackers
Serves 48

1-1/4	cups	Parmesan cheese -- grated
1	cup	Fearn® Soya Powder
1/2	cup	butter -- softened
1	teaspoon	xanthan gum
3/4	teaspoon	dried marjoram
3/4	teaspoon	dried oregano
3/4	teaspoon	basil -- chopped
1/2	teaspoon	Worcestershire sauce
		water

In medium mixing bowl, combine cheese, soya powder, butter, xanthan gum and herbs. Blend until mixture resembles coarse meal. Add Worcestershire sauce and just enough water to form the dough into a ball. Roll dough into a 1-1/2 inch thick cylinder. Wrap dough in plastic and chill 1-2 hours until firm. Slice dough into 1/4 inch slices. Place on greased cookie sheet.

Bake at 350° for 12-15 minutes or just until lightly brown.

Per serving: 0.8 g carbohydrates   34.8 calories
              0.4 g fiber   2.9 g fat
                                     1.7 g protein

Wheat Germ - Cheese Bars
Serves 16

1/2	pound	sharp cheddar cheese -- shredded
1	cup	Fearn® Soya Powder
1/4	cup	wheat germ
1/2	teaspoon	baking powder
1/4	teaspoon	salt
1/8	teaspoon	cayenne pepper
1	teaspoon	xanthan gum
3	tablespoons	oil
1/8	cup	half & half
1/8	cup	water
1/3	cup	walnuts -- finely chopped

In medium mixing bowl, combine the cheese with the soya powder, coating evenly. Add the wheat germ, baking powder, salt, pepper and xanthan gum. Mix well. Blend in the liquid ingredients. Add the walnuts. Press the mixture into a greased 8x8 baking dish.

Bake at 350° for 20-25 minutes. Cool before cutting into 16 squares.

Per serving: 3.3 g carbohydrates   128.9 calories
               1.4 g fiber   10.3 g fat
                                           7.1 g protein

Herb and Cheese Muffins
Serves 12

1/4	cup	Fearn® soya powder — sifted
3/4	cup	almond flour — see page 25
5/8	cup	Bob's Red Mill® Vital Wheat Gluten Flour
1/2	teaspoon	garlic powder
1/2	teaspoon	salt
1/8	teaspoon	thyme
1/8	teaspoon	basil
1/8	teaspoon	marjoram
1/4	teaspoon	parsley
3	teaspoons	baking powder
1	teaspoon	xanthan gum
3		eggs
2	tablespoons	oil
1/2	cup	whipping cream
1/4	cup	water
2	teaspoons	butter extract
4	ounces	cheddar cheese — shredded

Combine all dry ingredients in medium mixing bowl. Combine all wet ingredients in separate mixing bowl. Add wet ingredients to dry ingredients. Mix well. Add shredded cheese. Place in sprayed 12-cup muffin tins.

Bake at 375° for 15 minutes.

Per serving: 4.7 g carbohydrates   180.6 calories
              0.5 g fiber   13.9 g fat
                                     10.8 g protein

Favorite Recipes

SOUPS and SAUCES

Bean and Sausage Soup
Caesar Dressing
Chili with Beans
Cauliflower Soup
Cheese "Potato" Soup
Cheese Soup
Cheeseburger Soup
Cheese Sauce
Clam Chowder
Hollandaise Sauce
Tuscan Bean Soup with Sausage

Fast & Easy Tips

- For a quick soup, try chicken bouillon with canned chicken.

- Canned soup is fast but the carb counts are high. Try eating a very small portion as a side instead of as the meal itself.

- Five Brothers® Alfredo Sauce in a jar is not only fast and easy but wonderful. At only 2 grams carb per 1/4 cup, put it on everything.

- If the half & half or sour cream in your soup separates or curdles from overheating, strain the liquid into the blender. Blend for a minutes and return to the soup.

- It's easy to convert any recipe calling for milk – for every cup of milk, substitute 1/2 cup half & half and 1/2 cup water.

SOUPS and SAUCES

Bean and Sausage Soup
Serves 6

15	ounces	Eden® black soybeans -- rinsed and drained
5	cans	Swanson's® Fat-Free Chicken Broth
1/2	cup	onion -- chopped
1/4	cup	green pepper -- chopped
1	teaspoon	garlic -- minced
1		carrot -- pared, sliced thin
2		celery stalks -- sliced thin
2	tablespoons	butter
1	tablespoon	guar gum
1	tablespoon	white wine vinegar
1	pound	Hillshire Farms® Beef Smoked Sausage -- sliced
		salt -- to taste
		pepper -- to taste

In large sauce pan, combine beans, 4 cans of chicken broth, onion, green pepper, garlic, carrot and celery. Bring to boil, turn heat down to simmer, cover and cook for 30 minutes.

In small skillet, melt butter, add guar gum and 1 can chicken stock. Whisk together until thick, smooth paste is formed. Stir mixture into the hot soup. Add vinegar and sausage slices. Cover and simmer for 10 minutes. Season with salt and pepper before serving.

Per serving: 9.6 g carbohydrates   375.5 calories
               5.6 g fiber   29.8 g fat
                                        16.6 g protein

Caesar Dressing
Serves 6

2	tablespoons	lemon juice
1/2	tablespoon	garlic — minced
1	teaspoon	Worcestershire sauce
		black pepper — to taste
1	teaspoon	Dijon mustard
2	tablespoons	oil
1/4	cup	sour cream

In a small bowl, whisk together lemon juice, garlic, Worcestershire sauce, pepper, mustard and oil until blended. Add sour cream and mix well.

Per serving: 1.1 g carbohydrates   63.2 calories
              0.0 g fiber   6.6 g fat
                                           0.4 g protein

Chili with Beans
Serves 4

1	pound	ground beef
15	ounces	Eden® black soybeans -- rinsed and drained
4	ounces	tomato sauce
4	ounces	water
2	teaspoons	chili powder
		salt -- to taste
4	tablespoons	cheddar cheese -- shredded

Brown ground beef in skillet. Drain off excess fat. In medium sauce pan, mix ground beef, soybeans, tomato sauce, water and seasonings. Cook over medium heat for about 10 minutes. Top bowls of chili with shredded cheese just before serving.

Per serving: 9.4 g carbohydrates   409.9 calories
              6.6 g fiber   37.7 g fat
                                           30.1 g protein

Cauliflower Soup
Serves 8

2	cups	cauliflower
2	cups	water
1	stalk	celery -- chopped
1/2	cup	onion -- chopped
1	tablespoon	lemon juice
2	tablespoons	butter
2	teaspoons	guar gum
2-1/2	cups	water
1		chicken bouillon cube
1/2	cup	whipping cream
3/4	teaspoon	salt
1/8	teaspoon	pepper
	dash	nutmeg

Steam cauliflower and separate into flowerets. Heat 2 cups of water to boiling in large saucepan. Add cauliflower, celery, onion and lemon juice. Cook for 10 minutes or until tender. Remove cauliflower with slotted spoon and place in blender or food processor. Blend until smooth. Return to pan. Add butter, guar gum, remaining water and bouillon cube. Heat until soup thickens. Stir in whipping cream and seasonings. Heat through but do not boil.

Per serving: 2.3 g carbohydrates   84.8 calories
              1.0 g fiber   8.4 g fat
                                       0.7 g protein

SOUPS and SAUCES

Cheese "Potato" Soup
Serves 4

2	cups	cauliflower -- chopped
1/2	cup	onion -- chopped
1-1/2	cups	water
2		chicken bouillon cube
8	ounces	Velveeta® Cheese loaf -- cubed
4	slices	bacon -- cooked and chopped

Heat cauliflower, onion, water and bouillon to boiling in large pan. Cover and cook about 10 minutes or until cauliflower is tender. Pour mixture and cheese in blender or food processor. Cover and mix until smooth. Pour into 4 bowls and top with crumbled bacon.

Per serving: 8.5 g carbohydrates   232.1 calories
               0.8 g fiber   15.5 g fat
                                           13.0 g protein

Cheese Soup
Serves 3

2	tablespoons	butter
3	tablespoons	green onion -- chopped
1	stalk	celery -- chopped
1-1/4	cups	water
1/2	cup	half & half
2/3	cup	Velveeta® Cheese loaf -- cubed
1		chicken bouillon cube
1/3	cup	dry white wine -- optional
1/8	teaspoon	nutmeg

Melt butter in skillet. Add onions and celery and cook for about 8 minutes. Stir in water, half & half, cheese, bouillon and nutmeg. Heat until boiling, stirring constantly. Stir in wine. Return to boil for 1 minute. Pour into 3 bowls and garnish with nutmeg.

Per serving: 8.9 g carbohydrates   313.8 calories
               0.4 g fiber   23.6 g fat
                                           11.1 g protein

SOUPS and SAUCES

Cheeseburger Soup
Serves 6

1	tablespoon	oil
1	teaspoon	garlic -- minced
1/2	cup	onion -- chopped
1	stalk	celery -- sliced
1/2	cup	green pepper -- chopped
12	ounces	ground beef
1		beef bouillon cube -- crushed
2	cups	whipping cream
6	ounces	sharp cheddar cheese -- shredded

Heat the oil in a medium soup pot. Cook garlic, onion, celery and green pepper until tender. Add ground beef and stir until browned. Add the bouillon cube. Stirring constantly, slowly add the whipping cream. Do not let mixture boil. Add cheese and stir only until melted. Serve immediately.

Per serving: 4.0 g carbohydrates   590.5 calories
              0.4 g fiber   56.1 g fat
                                          18.5 g protein

Cheese Sauce
Serves 3

2	tablespoons	butter
2	tablespoons	oat flour — see page 25
1	cup	half & half
2	ounces	Swiss cheese — cubed
		salt — to taste

Melt butter in sauce pan. Stir in oat flour. Cook for 2 minutes, stirring constantly. Add half & half and continue to cook over low heat, stirring until sauce bubbles. Add cheese. Cook until cheese melts. Add salt. Serve warm.

Per serving: 6.6 g carbohydrates   258.2 calories
              0.5 g fiber   22.3 g fat
                                          8.5 g protein

SOUPS and SAUCES

Clam Chowder
Serves 16

1-1/2	tablespoons	bacon drippings
1	cup	onion -- chopped
4	cups	cauliflower -- chopped
3	pounds	clams -- with juice
4	cups	half & half
4	cups	whipping cream
		salt -- to taste
		pepper -- to taste

Heat drippings in medium soup pot. Cook onion until translucent. Add cauliflower, clam juice, half & half and whipping cream. Cook over medium heat for 20 minutes. Add clams and stir. (Do not cook too long, clams will become tough.) Salt and pepper. Serve warm.

Per serving: 7.4 g carbohydrates   362.4 calories
               0.4 g fiber   31.1 g fat
                                       4.2 g protein

Hollandaise Sauce
Serves 3

2		egg yolks -- slightly beaten
3	tablespoons	lemon juice
1/2	cup	butter

In small pan, stir egg yolks and lemon juice vigorously. Add 1/4 cup butter. Heat over low heat, stirring constantly, until butter has melted. Add remaining butter and stir until melted and sauce thickens. Serve hot.

Per serving: 1.6 g carbohydrates   311.0 calories
               0.1 g fiber   33.7 g fat
                                       2.2 g protein

Tuscan Bean Soup with Sausage
Serves 4

1	tablespoon	oil
1/4	pound	Hillshire Farms® Beef Smoked Sausage -- sliced
2	teaspoons	fennel seeds
1/2	cup	onion -- chopped
2	cups	cabbage -- shredded
2	cloves	garlic -- minced
15	ounces	Eden® black soybeans
2	cans	Swanson's® Fat-Free Chicken Broth
1	cup	Italian tomatoes -- stewed

Warm oil in a large saucepan over medium heat. Add sausage and fennel seeds. Cook 10 minutes, or until sausage is no longer pink. Remove sausage to a small bowl, leaving drippings in the saucepan. Add onion and garlic to drippings. Cook 5 minutes, or until onion is tender. Stir in beans, broth, tomatoes and sausage. Heat to boiling. Reduce heat to low, cover and simmer 20 minutes.

Per serving: 13.3 g carbohydrates   257.1 calories
              7.5 g fiber   17.2 g fat
                                     14.4 g protein

Favorite Recipes

BREAKFAST DISHES

"French Toast" Eggs
Cream of "Wheat"
Granola
Strawberry Jam
Ham and Egg "Cupcakes"
Cottage Cheese Pancakes
Ham and Cheese Roll
Pancakes
Sausage Spinach Bake
Chili-Cheese Oven Omelet

Fast & Easy Tips

- Be creative – add anything you desire to scrambled eggs. Add leftover vegetables or leftover meats.

- Who said you had to eat eggs for breakfast? Have a steak or ham or chicken.

- Craving cereal? Try not/Cereal® from Expert Foods (see page 16).

- Protein drinks are very fast and easy for breakfast. Many brands ands flavors are available. Try Atkins, Carbolite or Designer Whey Protein mixes. Be sure to check labels for carb counts on other brands.

- Any recipe calling for milk can be easily substituted. 1 cup milk = 1/2 cup half & half and 1/2 cup water.

BREAKFAST DISHES

"French Toast" Eggs
Serves 1

1		egg
2	tablespoons	Frigo® ricotta, part skim
1	teaspoon	vanilla extract
	dash	cinnamon
	dash	nutmeg
1	packet	sugar substitute — see page 21
	dash	salt
1	tablespoon	butter -- melted

Combine all ingredients in small mixing bowl. Whisk until blended well. Melt butter in skillet. Pour cheese mixture into melted butter. Carefully flip when first side has set and turned slightly golden.

Note: Softened cream cheese can be substituted for the ricotta cheese, if desired.

Per serving: 3.0 g carbohydrates　　212.4 calories
　　　　　　　0.0 g fiber　　　　　　　18.1 g fat
　　　　　　　　　　　　　　　　　　　8.9 g protein

Cream of "Wheat"
Serves 1

1/2	cup	Frigo® ricotta, part skim
3	tablespoons	whipping cream
1		egg
1	teaspoon	vanilla extract
1	packet	sugar substitute — see page 21
1/2	teaspoon	cinnamon

Combine all ingredients in a small pan. Mix well. Stir over medium heat just until boiling. Reduce heat and stir until desired thickness. Serve warm.

Per serving: 8.1 g carbohydrates　　388.8 calories
　　　　　　　0.6 fiber　　　　　　　30.8 g fat
　　　　　　　　　　　　　　　　　　20.3 g protein

BREAKFAST DISHES

Granola
Serves 7

6		Bran-a-crisp® crackers
1/2	cup	macadamia nuts -- coarsely chopped
1/2	cup	walnuts -- coarsely chopped
1/4	cup	Kroger® unsweetened coconut -- flaked
1	cup	puffed wheat cereal
1/3	cup	sugar substitute — see page 21
1/2	teaspoon	vanilla extract
3	tablespoons	butter -- melted

Break Bran-a-crisps® into 1/2" bite-sized pieces. Add chopped nuts, coconut and puffed wheat. Mix well. In separate bowl, combine sugar substitute, vanilla and melted butter. Pour melted mixture over dry mixture. Mix well. Spread evenly on ungreased cookie sheet.

Bake at 300° for 10 minutes. Stir mixture and bake an additional 10 minutes. Be careful not to over cook. Cool before serving.

Per serving: 9.3 g carbohydrates   201.7 calories
               4.8 g fiber   12.4 g fat
                                            3.2 g protein

Strawberry Jam
Serves 40

8	cups	strawberries -- crushed
5	cups	sugar substitute — see page 21
2	teaspoons	not/Sugar®
2	tablespoons	lemon juice

Mix ingredients in heavy pan. Heat to boiling over high heat, stirring frequently. Continue boiling and stirring until translucent and thick, about 25 minutes. Pour into sterilized jars. Seal according to lid directions. Makes 5 half-pint jars.

Per serving: 5.1 g carbohydrates   20.8 calories
               0.7 g fiber   0.1 g fat
                                            0.2 g protein

Ham and Egg "Cupcakes"
Serves 6

6	slices	ham slices -- thinly sliced
6		eggs
1	tablespoon	half & half
1/2	teaspoon	salt
1/2	teaspoon	pepper
3	tablespoons	fresh mushrooms -- sliced
1/4	cup	onion -- chopped
1/2	cup	cheddar cheese -- shredded

Grease or spray 6 cup muffin tin. Place one ham slice in each cup. In separate bowl, combine eggs, half & half, salt, pepper, mushrooms, onion and cheese. Mix well. Spoon about 1/2 cup of mixture into each ham cup. Use all mixture.

Bake at 375° for 20-25 minutes.

Per serving: 1.2 g carbohydrates   155.0 calories
              0.2 g fiber   11.3 g fat
                                      11.5 g protein

Cottage Cheese Pancakes
Serves 4

3		eggs -- beaten
1	cup	cottage cheese, small curd
2	tablespoons	oil
1/4	cup	oat flour — see page 25
1/2	teaspoon	salt

Combine all ingredients in small mixing bowl. Heat oiled griddle. Spoon batter into hot oil. Turn over to brown both sides.

Per serving: 6.7 g carbohydrates   185.4 calories
              1.0 g fiber   12.6 g fat
                                      11.4 g protein

Ham and Cheese Roll
Serves 6

16		eggs
4	ounces	cream cheese -- softened
1	cup	ham -- diced
4	ounces	canned mushrooms -- drained
3/4	cup	cheddar cheese -- shredded
3/4	cup	Swiss cheese -- shredded
		salt -- to taste
		pepper -- to taste

In medium bowl, beat eggs well with whisk. Line 15x10 pan with parchment paper. Spray with non-stick cooking spray. Pour eggs in pan.

Bake at 350° for 12-14 minutes or until eggs are set.

In separate bowls, cream cheese, ham and mushrooms in microwave. Line a cookie sheet with foil. Place over pan with cooked eggs. Flip over to place eggs on cookie sheet. Remove baking pan and parchment paper from eggs. Spread cream cheese on eggs. Evenly sprinkle ham and mushrooms over cream cheese. Starting at short end of foil, roll eggs into big roll. Remove foil from eggs as you roll. Place foil around completed roll on cookie sheet. Cut and serve after cheese melts.

Per serving:
- 4.2 g carbohydrates
- 0.5 g fiber
- 392.2 calories
- 29.1g fat
- 27.6 g protein

BREAKFAST DISHES

Pancakes
Serves 2

2-1/2	tablespoons	Bob's Red Mill® Vital Wheat Gluten Flour
2	tablespoons	whipping cream
1	tablespoon	water
1	tablespoon	oil
1/2	teaspoon	baking powder
2		eggs
1	teaspoon	sugar substitute — see page 21
1/2	teaspoon	cinnamon

In small mixing bowl, mix all ingredients with fork. Blend until smooth with wire whip. Pour 1/2 mixture into skillet with heated oil. Turn when bottom is set and slightly golden. Remove when done. Repeat with rest of mixture.

Per serving: 3.8 g carbohydrates   215.4 calories
              0.3 g fiber   16.8 g fat
                                         12.8 g protein

Sausage Spinach Bake
Serves 8

1	pound	Hillshire Farms® Beef Smoked Sausage -- sliced
6		eggs
20	ounces	frozen spinach -- thawed and drained
16	ounces	Mozzarella cheese -- shredded
1/3	cup	Frigo® ricotta, part skim
1/2	teaspoon	salt
1/8	teaspoon	pepper
1/8	teaspoon	garlic powder

In medium skillet, cook sausage until well browned. Drain. In separate bowl, combine eggs, spinach, cheeses and seasonings. Add sausage and pour into baking dish.

Bake at 350° for 40-45 minutes.

Per serving: 6.0 g carbohydrates   448.8 calories
              2.1 g fiber   35.2 g fat
                                     26.5 g protein

Chili-Cheese Oven Omelet
Serves 8

2	cups	cheddar cheese -- shredded
4	ounces	green chilies -- drained
2	cups	Monterey jack cheese -- shredded
1/2	cup	half & half
3/4	cup	water
3	tablespoons	Fearn® Soya Powder
1/2	teaspoon	salt
3		eggs
8	ounces	tomato sauce

Layer cheddar cheese, chilies and Monterey jack cheese in greased square baking dish (8x8x2). In separate bowl, combine half & half, water, soya powder, salt and eggs. Pour mixture over cheese layers.

Bake uncovered at 350° for about 40 minutes, or until set in center. Let stand 10 minutes before cutting. Heat tomato sauce and serve with omelet.

Per serving: 6.0 g carbohydrates   448.8 calories
               2.1 g fiber   35.2 g fat
                                           26.5 g protein

Favorite Recipes

Salads

Coleslaw
Pickled Beets
Spinach Salad
Wilted Lettuce Salad
Sauerkraut Slaw
Bacon - Cauliflower Toss
Florentine Salad
Fresh Mushroom Salad
Mushroom - Spinach Toss
Green Bean Salad

Fast & Easy Tips

- Grocery stores carry ready-to-eat salads in a bag. Watch out for the croutons.

- Most salad dressings are low in carbs. Read the labels. Don't get the low fat versions – they are higher in carbs.

- Get real bacon bits (0 carbs).

- Watch out for carrots. They are high in carbs – 1/2 cup shredded is 5.6 grams carb.

- Forget those rules you grew up with. You know the ones – always serve this with this and that with that. Be creative!

SALADS

Coleslaw
Serves 12

1/3	cup	sugar substitute — see page 21
1/2	teaspoon	salt
1/8	teaspoon	pepper
1/2	cup	Hellman's® mayonnaise
1/4	cup	half & half
1-1/2	tablespoons	white vinegar
2-1/2	tablespoons	lemon juice
8	cups	cabbage -- chopped fine
1		carrot -- chopped

Combine sugar substitute, salt, pepper, mayonnaise, half a& half, vinegar and lemon juice. Add cabbage and carrot. Mix well. Cover and refrigerate for 2 hours before serving.

Per serving: 5.1 g carbohydrates   94.4 calories
              1.5 g fiber   8.1 g fat
                                         1.1 g protein

Pickled Beets
Serves 16

32	ounces	beets, canned
1-1/2	cups	sugar substitute — see page 21
3/4	cup	vinegar
2		cinnamon sticks -- 3 inch each

Drain beets, reserving liquid in a saucepan. Place beets in a medium bowl. Add sugar substitute, vinegar and cinnamon sticks to reserved liquid. Heat to boiling, stirring constantly. Pour liquid over beets. Let cool. Cover and refrigerate at least 8 hours before serving.

Per serving: 8.1 g carbohydrates   31.5 calories
              1.5 g fiber   0.1 g fat
                                         0.5 g protein

Spinach Salad
Serves 4

4	slices	bacon
1-1/2	cups	romaine lettuce
1-1/2	cups	spinach leaves
4		eggs -- hard boiled
1/3	cup	red onion -- sliced
2	stalks	celery -- thinly sliced
4	ounces	sour cream
1	tablespoon	half & half
2	tablespoons	sugar substitute — see page 21
1	tablespoon	red wine vinegar
1/2	teaspoon	salt
1/4	teaspoon	pepper

Cook bacon until crisp and crumble when cooled. In medium mixing bowl, shred lettuce and spinach into bite sized pieces. Slice hard boiled eggs and add to lettuce. Add bacon, onion and celery to lettuce. In separate bowl, mix sour cream, half & half, sugar substitute, vinegar and seasonings. Add dressing to salad and mix well.

Per serving:
>5.7 g carbohydrates
>1.5 g fiber

>183.3 calories
>13.9 g fat
>9.3 g protein

Wilted Lettuce Salad
Serves 4

4	slices	bacon
1/4	cup	vinegar
4	cups	lettuce -- shredded
1/3	cup	scallions -- chopped
2	teaspoons	sugar substitute — see page 21
1/4	teaspoon	salt
1/8	teaspoon	pepper

Fry bacon until crisp. Let cool and chop into small pieces. Add vinegar to skillet and heat bacon pieces. In separate bowl mix lettuce and onions. Pour vinegar and bacon over lettuce. Add sugar substitute, salt and pepper. Toss until lettuce is wilted.

Per serving: 3.1 g carbohydrates   48.8 calories
                0.9 g fiber   3.3 g fat
                                           2.6 g protein

Sauerkraut Slaw
Serves 8

16	ounces	sauerkraut -- drained
1	cup	celery -- sliced
1/4	cup	green pepper -- sliced
1/2	cup	onion -- chopped
1/4	cup	sugar substitute — see page 21
1/3	cup	sour cream
1/2	teaspoon	celery seed

Chop sauerkraut into small pieces. In medium bowl, mix sauerkraut, celery, green pepper, onion, sugar substitute, sour cream and celery seed. Cover and chill for at least 24 hours. Stir occasionally.

Per serving: 4.7 g carbohydrates   39.6 calories
                1.9 g fiber   2.2 g fat
                                           1.0 g protein

Bacon - Cauliflower Toss
Serves 4

2	cups	Romaine lettuce — torn
8	slices	bacon -- fried and crumbled
2	cups	cauliflower flowerets
1/4	cup	radishes -- sliced
1/4	cup	Hellman's® mayonnaise
1/4	cup	sour cream
2	tablespoons	scallions -- sliced
1/4	teaspoon	dried dill weed
		fresh ground pepper

Layer half of Romaine lettuce, half of bacon and half of cauliflower in salad bowl. Layer radishes. Repeat layers of lettuce, bacon and cauliflower.

In separate bowl, mix mayonnaise, sour cream and onions. Layer dressing over cauliflower in salad bowl. Sprinkle with dill and pepper. Cover and chill for at least 2 hours. Toss just before serving.

Per serving: 4.4 g carbohydrates   222.7 calories
               2.1 g fiber   20.4 g fat
                                           5.8 g protein

Florentine Salad
Serves 3

1	clove	garlic -- slivered
1/3	cup	oil
1/4	cup	wine vinegar
1/4	teaspoon	salt
	dash	pepper
12	ounces	spinach leaves -- torn
1		hard-boiled egg -- chopped
2	slices	bacon -- fried and crumbled

Let garlic slices stand in oil for 1 hour. Discard garlic slices. Mix oil, vinegar, salt and pepper in salad bowl. Add spinach leaves to oil and toss until well coated. Sprinkle with egg and bacon. Toss again.

Per serving: 4.5 g carbohydrates   282.5 calories
              2.2 g fiber   28.1 g fat
                                      5.5 g protein

Variation: Hot Florentine Salad - prepare as direct except heat oil, vinegar, salt and pepper over low heat. Stir constantly until hot.

Fresh Mushroom Salad
Serves 6

1	pound	fresh mushrooms
5	tablespoons	oil
2	tablespoons	wine vinegar
1/4	cup	fresh parsley -- chopped
1	teaspoon	dried tarragon
1/2	teaspoon	salt
1/8	teaspoon	pepper

Rinse mushrooms thoroughly in cold water. Remove the stems. Slice mushroom caps crosswise about 1/4 inch thick. In medium mixing bowl, mix mushrooms, oil, vinegar and seasonings. Toss well. Cover and chill for an hour before serving.

Per serving: 4.0 g carbohydrates   121.2 calories
               1.0 g fiber   11.7 g fat
                                           1.6 g protein

Mushroom - Spinach Toss
Serves 4

2	tablespoons	wine vinegar
3/4	teaspoon	salt
1	clove	garlic -- crushed
	dash	fresh ground pepper
8	ounces	mushrooms -- sliced
16	ounces	spinach leaves -- torn
1/4	cup	oil

Mix vinegar, salt, garlic and pepper. Toss with mushrooms. Let stand for about 15 minutes. In separate bowl, toss spinach leaves with oil until evenly coated. Add mushroom mixture to spinach and toss again.

Per serving: 6.1 g carbohydrates   154.2 calories
               2.9 g fiber   14.1 g fat
                                           3.5 g protein

Green Bean Salad
Serves 6

1	pound	green beans -- fresh
4	slices	bacon -- fried and crumbled
1/2	cup	red onion -- sliced
2	tablespoons	oil
1	tablespoon	sugar substitute -- see page 21
1/2	tablespoon	pepper
1/8	teaspoon	thyme
3	tablespoons	cider vinegar

Cut beans crosswise into 1" pieces. Cook in 1" of boiling water until tender-crisp, about 7 minutes. (Do not salt.) Drain and cool. Mix beans, bacon and onion. In separate bowl, combine remaining ingredients. Toss dressing with beans. Cover and refrigerate for 1 hour.

Per serving: 6.9 g carbohydrates   93.2 calories
               1.02.6 g fiber   6.7 g fat
                                          2.7 g protein

Favorite Recipes

VEGETABLES

Asparagus Casserole
Baked Beans
Broccoli with Pecans
"French Fries"
Fried Spinach
Green Beans with Dill Sauce
Mexican Spinach with Beans
Refried Beans
Mushroom Casserole
Posh Squash
"Potato" Casserole
Spinach Soufflé
Spinach Squares
Zucchini Parmesan
Zucchini Patties
Roasted Cauliflower with Coriander
Fried Eggplant

Fast & Easy Tips

- Stock up on frozen and canned vegetables.

- Learn to can your own green beans. You do the work once a year and then simply reheat.

- Vegetables fried in butter and seasoned with SPIKE® always work in my house.

- "No Sugar Added" simply means no table sugar added. Be sure to check the ingredients list for dextrose, fructose, sucrose, sorbitol, corn syrup or any other hidden carbs.

- Slice mushrooms with an egg slicing gizmo.

- Use only one third the amount of fresh herbs when substituting dried herbs.

Asparagus Casserole
Serves 6

3	tablespoons	butter
2	teaspoons	guar gum
3/4	cup	half & half
3/4	cup	water
2	cups	asparagus spears, canned -- cut in 1" pieces
8	ounces	mushrooms, canned -- drained
4	tablespoons	slivered almonds
2	tablespoons	pimiento -- chopped
1/2	cup	cheddar cheese -- shredded
		paprika

In medium saucepan, melt butter. Add guar gum and stir. Add half & half and water. Heat, stirring continuously, until thickened. Add asparagus, mushrooms, almonds and pimento to white sauce. Mix well. Pour into greased baking dish. Spread cheese over top.

Bake at 350° for 30 minutes. Sprinkle with paprika before serving.

Per serving: 7.3 g carbohydrates   190.6 calories
3.3 g fiber   16.1 g fat
     7.0 g protein

VEGETABLES

Baked Beans
Serves 6

60	ounces	Eden® black soybeans -- rinsed and drained
1/2	cup	onion -- chopped
1/4	pound	salt pork -- sliced thin
1/4	cup	sugar substitute — see page 21
1/2	teaspoon	maple extract
1	teaspoon	salt
1/4	teaspoon	dry mustard
1/8	teaspoon	pepper
1	cup	water

Layer beans, onion and salt pork in ungreased 3-4 quart baking dish. In separate bowl, mix sugar substitute, seasonings and water. Pour over beans.

Cook at 350° for 30 minutes.

Per serving: 19.1 g carbohydrates   410.5 calories
              15.5 g fiber   28.3 g fat
                                       25.1 g protein

Broccoli with Pecans
Serves 8

3	cups	broccoli flowerets
1	envelope	Kroger® Onion Soup Mix
1	cup	pecan halves
8	ounces	water chestnuts, canned -- drained
1/2	cup	butter -- melted

Spread broccoli in 9x13 baking dish. Pour butter over broccoli. In separate bowl, mix onion soup mix with pecans and water chestnuts. Sprinkle over broccoli.

Bake at 325° for 30 minutes. Toss before serving to evenly coat.

Per serving: 9.9 g carbohydrates   189.1 calories
              3.0 g fiber   16.4 g fat
                                      2.7 g protein

VEGETABLES

"French Fries"
Serves 2

		oil
1	cup	zucchini -- cut in 1/2" strips
1/3	cup	Fearn® Soya Powder
		Spike® seasoning
		salt -- to taste

Cut zucchini into strips resembling French fries. Dredge strips in soya powder, shaking off excess. Place in heated oil (approximately 375°). Remove with slotted spoon. They will cook quickly. Drain on paper towels. Sprinkle with Spike® and salt.

Per serving: 6.5 g carbohydrates   75.3 calories
              3.1 g fiber   3.4 g fat
                                          7.4 g protein

Variations: Try this with daikon radish or celeriac.

Fried Spinach
Serves 4

2	cups	frozen chopped spinach -- thawed
1		egg
1	tablespoon	wheat germ
		pepper -- to taste
1/4	teaspoon	nutmeg
1	tablespoon	butter
2	tablespoons	feta cheese -- grated

Cook the spinach in water until just wilted. Drain any liquid. In mixing bowl, combine spinach, egg, wheat germ, pepper and nutmeg. Melt butter in skillet. Pour spinach mixture into skillet. Fry for 3 minutes. Carefully turn the pancake. Sprinkle top with feta cheese. Fry until bottom is slightly browned. Remove from skillet and cut into wedges before serving.

Per serving: 4.3 g carbohydrates   75.4 calories
              2.6 g fiber   5.1 g fat
                                          4.5 g protein

VEGETABLES

Green Beans with Dill Sauce
Serves 6

1	pound	green beans -- sliced 1-inch long
4	cloves	garlic -- unpeeled
4	ounces	tofu -- drained and diced
1/4	cup	lemon juice
2	teaspoons	Dijon mustard
1/4	cup	dill -- snipped
1/2	teaspoon	salt
1/2	cup	oil

Steam green beans and garlic cloves for 5-6 minutes, just until tender. Remove skins from garlic and place in blender or food processor. Add tofu, lemon juice, mustard, dill and salt. Mix well. While still blending mixture, slowly add oil until homogeneous. Pour sauce over warm green beans and toss before serving.

Per serving: 7.8 g carbohydrates   207.2 calories
              2.6 g fiber   19.3 g fat
                                      3.4 g protein

Mexican Spinach with Beans
Serves 4

2	tablespoons	bacon drippings
1	teaspoon	red pepper flakes
1/2	cup	onion -- chopped fine
1	teaspoon	garlic -- minced
1	package	frozen chopped spinach -- thawed
15	ounces	Eden® black soybeans -- rinsed and drained
1	teaspoon	vinegar

In large skillet, heat bacon drippings. Add red pepper flakes and chopped onion. Stir until onion is translucent. Add garlic. Stir for another 30 seconds. Add spinach, beans and vinegar. Stir for 10 minutes, stirring frequently. Serve warm.

Per serving: 10.5 g carbohydrates   179.4 calories
              8.1 g fiber   11.7 g fat
                                      11.3 g protein

Refried Beans
Serves 4

1/2	cup	onion -- chopped
1/4	cup	butter
30	ounces	Eden® black soybeans -- mashed
3/4	teaspoon	salt
1/2	cup	cheddar cheese -- shredded

In skillet, melt butter and add onion. Stir until translucent. Add remaining ingredients and mix well until heated through.

Per serving: 14.1 g carbohydrates   357.5 calories
              11.7 g fiber   25.9 g fat
                                      21.8 g protein

Mushroom Casserole
Serves 6

12	ounces	mushrooms -- sliced
1/4	cup	onion -- chopped
4	tablespoons	butter
1	teaspoon	Spike® seasoning
1/2	teaspoon	salt
1/3	cup	whipping cream
2		eggs
1	cup	Swiss cheese -- shredded

In skillet, sauté sliced mushrooms and onion in butter. Add Spike® and salt (or your favorite herbs) and cook for about 5 minutes. In a separate bowl, combine the whipping cream and eggs. Spread shredded Swiss cheese on bottom of 2 quart casserole dish. Layer mushroom mixture on top of cheese. Pour egg mixture over top.

Bake at 375° for 30 minutes or until set.

Per serving: 4.0 g carbohydrates   220.3 calories
              0.8 g fiber   19.3 g fat
                                    8.7 g protein

Posh Squash
Serves 16

1	cup	Hellman's® mayonnaise
1	cup	Parmesan cheese
1/2	cup	onion -- finely chopped
		salt -- to taste
		pepper -- to taste
4	tablespoons	butter -- melted
1		egg
2-1/2	pounds	yellow squash -- thinly sliced
3	ounces	pork rinds -- crushed

Combine mayonnaise, Parmesan cheese, onion, salt, pepper, butter and egg. Add sliced squash and mix well. Place in a greased 9X13 baking dish. Top with crush pork rinds.

Bake at 350° for 50 minutes or until top is browned.

Per serving: 3.4 g carbohydrates   196.6 calories
               1.3 g fiber   17.6 g fat
                                          6.7 g protein

"Potato" Casserole
Serves 8

4	cups	cauliflower
8	ounces	cream cheese -- softened
2	cups	sour cream
3	tablespoons	whipping cream
1/2	cup	onion -- chopped
2	cups	sharp cheddar cheese -- shredded
		salt -- to taste
		pepper -- to taste
6	ounces	pork rinds -- crushed

Cut cauliflower into small pieces and steam until soft (see page x). In medium mixing bowl, mash until slightly chunky. Add cream cheese, sour cream, whipping cream, onions, cheddar cheese and seasonings. Mix well. Top with pork rinds.

Bake at 350° for 30-35 minutes.

Per serving: 5.2 g carbohydrates   483.8 calories
               0.6 g fiber   41.0 g fat
                                          25.3 g protein

VEGETABLES
93

Spinach Soufflé
Serves 8

1	tablespoon	butter -- melted
1/2	cup	onion -- chopped
1	clove	garlic -- minced
8	ounces	cream cheese -- softened
8	ounces	farmer's cheese
		salt -- to taste
		pepper -- to taste
3		eggs
20	ounces	frozen chopped spinach -- thawed and drained
1/4	teaspoon	paprika
1/8	teaspoon	ground nutmeg

Melt butter in skillet. Add onion and garlic and cook until tender. In separate bowl, combine cream cheese, farmers cheese, salt and pepper. Mix well. Add onion mixture and mix again. Add eggs, one at a time, and blend after each one. Mix in spinach. Pour mixture into well greased 9 in baking dish. Sprinkle with paprika and nutmeg. Cover.

Bake at 325° for 30 minutes. Uncover and bake for an additional 15 minutes.

Per serving: 4.4 g carbohydrates   225.9 calories
               2.3 g fiber   17.2 g fat
                                           15.4 g protein

Spinach Squares
Serves 8

1	tablespoon	oil
1/2	cup	onion -- chopped
3	ounces	mushrooms -- chopped
1/2	cup	red bell pepper -- chopped
4	cups	fresh spinach -- chopped
4	ounces	cream cheese -- softened
4		eggs
1/4	cup	pork rinds -- crushed
2	tablespoons	sesame seeds
2	tablespoons	Parmesan cheese
1/4	teaspoon	salt

Heat oil in large skillet. Add onion, mushrooms and pepper. Cook 5 minutes, or until tender. Add spinach leaves and cook another 2 minutes, or until wilted. Remove from heat. In separate bowl, beat cream cheese until smooth. Add eggs, pork rinds and 1 TBSP. each of sesame seeds and Parmesan cheese. Stir mixture into spinach. Spread mixture into 9x9 baking dish. Sprinkle with remaining sesames seeds and Parmesan cheese.

Bake at 350° for 30 minutes.

Per serving: 2.9 g carbohydrates 168.5 calories
 0.9 fiber 13.2 g fat
 10.6 g protein

Zucchini Parmesan
Serves 6

4	cups	zucchini -- thinly sliced
1/2	cup	onion -- sliced
1	tablespoon	water
2	tablespoons	butter
1	teaspoon	salt
	dash	pepper
3	tablespoons	Parmesan cheese -- grated

In large skillet, combine zucchini, onion, water, butter, salt and pepper. Bring to boil over high heat. Lower heat, cover and simmer for 3 minutes. Uncover, raise heat to medium. Cook for 10 minutes, turning frequently. Sprinkle with cheese. Serve warm.

Per serving: 3.0 g carbohydrates   58.9 calories
              1.2 g fiber   4.7 g fat
                                    2.1 g protein

VEGETABLES

Zucchini Patties
Serves 4

2	cups	zucchini -- grated
2		eggs
1/4	cup	onion -- minced
1/4	cup	Fearn® soya powder
1/4	cup	Parmesan cheese
1/2	teaspoon	baking powder
		salt -- to taste
		pepper -- to taste
1/4	teaspoon	oregano
		oil
		butter -- melted

Remove as moisture as possible from grated zucchini by pressing between paper towels in a strainer. In a separate bowl, mix zucchini with eggs and onion. Add soya powder, cheese, baking powder and seasonings. Mix well. Shape into 4 patties and place into heated oil. Fry until lightly browned on both sides. Drizzle with melted butter.

Per serving: 4.6 g carbohydrates   90.6 calories
              1.8 g fiber   5.0 g fat
                                         8.1 g protein

Roasted Cauliflower with Coriander
Serves 4

3	cups	cauliflower flowerets
1	teaspoon	ground cumin
1	teaspoon	coriander seeds — crushed
1	teaspoon	mustard seeds — optional

Rinse and drain cauliflower flowerets. Pat dry with paper towels. Spray roasting pan with oil. Place cauliflower in a single layer in pan. Spray again with oil. In separate bowl, combine seasonings. Sprinkle mixture over cauliflower. Stir to coat.

Roast, uncovered at 450° for 15-20 minutes. (If cauliflower looks to be drying out during roasting, spray again with oil.)

Per serving: 4.7 g carbohydrates   26.2 calories
               2.0 g fiber   0.6 g fat
                                          1.9 g protein

Fried Eggplant
Serves 6

1	medium	eggplant
2		eggs-- beaten
1/2	cup	Parmesan cheese — grated
1/2	cup	almond flour — see page 25
		Salt — to taste
		Pepper — to taste
		oil

Cut eggplant into strips 1/2 inch thick. Place beaten eggs in flat container. In separate bowl, combine Parmesan cheese and almond flour. Dip eggplant slices in egg and then dredge in flour mixture. Fry in hot oil until golden brown. Turn to cook other side. Remove and drain on paper towels. Season to taste. Serve hot.

Per serving: 6.4 g carbohydrates   116.9 calories
               1.6 g fiber   7.8 g fat
                                          6.8 g protein

Favorite Recipes

ENTREES

Almond Chicken
Parmesan Chicken
Baked Cheesy Pork Chops
Cabbage "Noodles"
Beef Stroganoff
Cabbage Rolls
Cheesy Broiled Flounder
Chicken Dijon
Chicken Cacciatore
Fried Chicken
Chicken Excelsior
Chicken Fried "Rice"
Chicken Kiev
Chicken Rolls Almondine
Chicken with Garlic Butter
Coconut Shrimp
Crab Casserole
Crab Cakes
Creamy Chicken Packets
Fish Roll-Ups
Meatloaf
Pepper Steak Packets
Portabello Mushroom Burgers
Spicy Hamburgers
Seafood Casserole
Shrimp Creole
Shrimp and Artichokes
Shrimp Foo Young
Stuffed Peppers
Stuffed Portabella Mushrooms
Taco Bake
Taco Meat

Fast & Easy Tips

- Stock up on easy to use items such as canned tuna, chicken, chicken broth, salmon, mushrooms, Five Brothers® Alfredo Sauce.

- Look for individually frozen chicken breasts in your freezer section.

- Keep a few protein drinks and bars on hand - they're great when you're in a hurry but need to eat.

- Eating out for dinner? Look for Caesar's salad with grilled chicken, any unbreaded meats, steamed vegetables, cheeseburgers (don't eat the bun), steak, etc. You can be choosy on a buffet.

- The best steak sauce ever invented is melted butter. All the "high end" restaurants use it.

Almond Chicken
Serves 2

1/4	cup	almond flour — see page 25
1	tablespoon	bread crumbs
1	tablespoon	Parmesan cheese
1/8	teaspoon	salt
1/8	teaspoon	basil
2		chicken breast halves without skin
1	tablespoon	half & half
2	tablespoons	oil

In medium bowl, combine almond flour, bread crumbs, cheese and seasonings. Dip chicken in half & half then coat with flour mixture. Heat oil in skillet before adding chicken. Cook 3-4 minutes per side, turning once.

Per serving: 6.3 g carbohydrates   352.9 calories
               0.2 g fiber   23.3 g fat
                                          30.0 g protein

Parmesan Chicken
Serves 4

4		chicken breast halves without skin
4	tablespoons	Hellman's® mayonnaise
6	tablespoons	Parmesan cheese
1/2	teaspoon	Italian seasoning
1/2	teaspoon	garlic powder
		salt -- to taste
		pepper -- to taste

Place cleaned chicken breasts in 8 " baking dish. In separate bowl, mix mayonnaise, cheese and seasonings. Spread mixture evenly on chicken breasts.

Bake at 350° for 45 minutes.

Per serving: 0.6 g carbohydrates   258.9 calories
               0.0 g fiber   14.6 g fat
                                          29.0 g protein

Baked Cheesy Pork Chops
Serves 6

6		pork chops
1	tablespoon	butter
1/2	cup	half & half
1/4	cup	water
8	ounces	cream cheese -- cubed
1	teaspoon	garlic salt
		pepper -- to taste
1/2	cup	Parmesan cheese

In skillet, brown pork chops in melted butter. In medium saucepan, heat half & half, water, cream cheese, garlic salt, pepper and half of Parmesan cheese. Mix well. Place pork chops in baking dish. Pour cheese sauce over chops. Sprinkle remaining Parmesan cheese on top.

Bake at 325° for 50 minutes.

Per serving: 2.1 g carbohydrates   437.0 calories
               0.0 g fiber   34.1 g fat
                                          29.3 g protein

Cabbage "Noodles"
Serves 4

3	cups	cabbage -- sliced
2	tablespoons	half & half
		water

Slice cabbage to create long thin strips. In large pan, bring water to boil. Add half & half and cabbage. Boil until cabbage is limp. Drain. Serve as noodles with desired topping or sauce.

Per serving: 3.9 g carbohydrates   26.6 calories
               1.5 g fiber   1.0 g fat
                                          1.2 g protein

Beef Stroganoff
Serves 6

1-1/2	pounds	sirloin steak -- cubed
2	tablespoons	butter
8	ounces	mushrooms -- sliced
1/2	cup	onion -- chopped
1-1/2	cups	beef bouillon
2	tablespoons	tomato paste
1	clove	garlic -- finely chopped
1	cup	sour cream
2	teaspoons	guar gum
		salt -- to taste
		pepper -- to taste

Cook meat in large skillet with butter until done. Stir in mushrooms and onion. Sauté until onions are translucent. Add 1 cup of bouillon, tomato paste, garlic and salt. Bring to a boil. Reduce heat. In a separate bowl, combine sour cream, remaining bouillon and guar gum. Add to the meat mixture. Bring to a boil again and reduce heat to simmer. Stir until mixture thickens. Season as needed.

Per serving: 6.2 g carbohydrates   373.6 calories
              1.5 g fiber   28.4 g fat
                                     23.3 g protein

Cabbage Rolls
Serves 12

12		cabbage leaves -- * see note below
1	pound	ground beef
1/2	cup	cauliflower -- cooked and chopped
1/2	cup	onion -- chopped
4	ounces	mushroom -- canned
1	teaspoon	salt
1/8	teaspoon	pepper
1/8	teaspoon	garlic salt
15	ounces	tomato sauce -- canned
1	teaspoon	sugar substitute — see page 21
1/2	teaspoon	lemon juice

*Note: to remove cabbage leaves from head: Remove the core. Place cabbage in large pan and cover with water. Let stand for 10 minutes. Carefully remove leaves.

Place cabbage leaves in large pan of boiling water. Cover and remove from heat. Let stand for 10 minutes or until leaves are limp. Remove leaves and drain. In separate bowl, mix ground beef, cauliflower, onion, mushrooms with liquid, seasonings and 1/2 cup of tomato sauce. Place about 1/3 cup mixture near the stem end of each cabbage leaf. Be sure to use all of mixture in the 12 leaves. Roll leaf around ground beef mixture, tucking in sides. Place cabbage rolls (seam side down) in ungreased 8x8 baking dish. Mix remaining tomato sauce with sugar substitute and lemon juice. Pour over cabbage rolls.

Cover and bake at 350° for about 45 minutes or until hamburger is done.

Per serving: 3.8 g carbohydrates   134.0 calories
              0.9 g fiber   10.2 g fat
                                       7.2 g protein

Cheesy Broiled Flounder
Serves 4

2	pounds	flounder
2	tablespoons	lemon juice
1/2	cup	Parmesan cheese
1/4	cup	butter -- softened
3	tablespoons	Hellman's® mayonnaise
1/4	cup	scallions -- chopped
1/4	teaspoon	salt
	dash	hot sauce

Place a single layer of fish fillets in a shallow broiler pan. Brush with lemon juice. In separate bowl, combine Parmesan cheese, butter, mayonnaise, scallions, salt and hot sauce. Set aside. Broil fillets for 406 minutes, or until fish flakes easily. remove from oven and spread cheese mixture on fillets. Broil for an additional 30 seconds.

Per serving: 1.5 g carbohydrates   379.1 calories
0.2 fiber   23.8 g fat
38.2 g protein

Chicken Dijon
Serves 4

4	tablespoons	Dijon mustard
2	tablespoons	oil
1	teaspoon	garlic powder
1/2	teaspoon	dried Italian seasoning
4		chicken breast halves without skin

In plastic bag, combine mustard, oil and seasonings. Add chicken to bag and move around to coat. Place coated chicken in greased baking dish.

Bake at 375° for 20 minutes.

Per serving: 1.6 g carbohydrates   197.4 calories
0.4 g fiber   8.9 g fat
26.7 g protein

Chicken Cacciatore
Serves 4

4		chicken breast halves without skin
1/2	cup	onion -- sliced
1/2	cup	green pepper -- sliced
8	ounces	canned mushrooms -- rinsed and drained
2	cups	Classico® pasta sauce
		salt -- to taste
		pepper -- to taste
1/2	teaspoon	basil

Place all ingredients in crockpot. Cook for 6-8 hours.

Per serving: 12.4 g carbohydrates   213.8 calories
               3.8 g fiber   4.6 g fat
                                            30.2 g protein

Fried Chicken
Serves 4

2		eggs
2	tablespoons	whipping cream
6	ounces	pork rinds -- crushed
1/2	cup	Parmesan cheese
2	teaspoons	garlic powder
		salt -- to taste
		pepper -- to taste
4		chicken breast halves without skin
2	tablespoons	oil

In medium bowl, mix egg and whipping cream well. In separate bowl, mix pork rinds, cheese and seasonings. Dip chicken in egg mixture, then dredge in pork rinds mixture. Heat oil in skillet. Place chicken in hot oil and cook until juices run clear, turning as necessary.

Per serving: 1.9 g carbohydrates   534.0 calories
               0.0 g fiber   31.3 g fat
                                            60.4 g protein

Chicken Excelsior
Serves 4

	dash	garlic salt
1/2	cup	butter -- melted
1	teaspoon	paprika
3	tablespoons	lemon juice
4		chicken breast halves without skin
1	cup	sour cream
1/2	cup	Swanson's® Fat-Free Chicken Broth
8	ounces	canned mushrooms -- drained
		pepper -- to taste

In small bowl mix garlic salt, butter, paprika and lemon juice. Place chicken breasts in shallow baking dish. Pour butter over chicken. In separate bowl, combine sour cream, broth, mushrooms and pepper. Set aside.

Bake, covered, at 375° for 30 minutes. Pour sauce over chicken and bake for another 15 minutes.

Per serving: 6.7 g carbohydrates   467.2 calories
              1.5 g fiber   36.4 g fat
                                       29.3 g protein

Chicken Fried "Rice"
Serves 3

		oil
1	teaspoon	sesame oil
3		chicken breast halves without skin -- cubed
2	cups	cauliflower -- grated
3		green onion -- chopped
1	tablespoon	soy sauce
2	cloves	garlic -- minced
1/2	teaspoon	salt
3		eggs -- beaten

Heat oil in wok or large skillet. Add chicken pieces and stir until done. Remove and add cauliflower and onion. Cook approximately 5 minutes, stirring constantly. Add soy sauce, garlic, salt and cooked chicken. Mix well. Move mixture to side and scramble eggs in oil. Mix all ingredients.

Per serving: 13.5 g carbohydrates   258.0 calories
                4.5 g fiber   7.5 g fat
                                              28.9 g protein

Variation: Substitute steak, shrimp or pork for chicken. Add broccoli, bean sprouts or water chestnuts.

Chicken Kiev
Serves 2

1/2	cup	pork rinds -- crushed
2	tablespoons	Parmesan cheese
1	teaspoon	dried basil
1	teaspoon	dried oregano
1/2	teaspoon	garlic powder
		salt -- to taste
		pepper -- to taste
2		chicken breast halves without skin
2/3	cup	butter -- melted

Mix pork rinds, Parmesan cheese and seasonings in medium bowl. Dip chicken in butter then coat with pork rinds mixture.

Place in baking dish. Bake at 375° for 45 minutes. Turn and cook for an additional 10 minutes. OR Place in skillet and fry until done, turning to cook both sides.

Per serving:
1.7 g carbohydrates
0.3 g fiber

1027.5 calories
84.7 g fat
66.9 g protein

Chicken Rolls Almondine
Serves 2

4	slices	bacon
1	teaspoon	chives
1/3	cup	fresh mushrooms -- sliced
1/4	cup	almonds -- toasted and chopped
1/4	teaspoon	dried thyme
2		chicken breast halves without skin
		salt -- to taste
		pepper -- to taste

In a medium baking dish, cook bacon in microwave until crisp. Drain, reserving 2 tablespoons of drippings. Add chives and mushrooms to reserved bacon drippings. Cover and microwave on high for 45-60 seconds until tender. Add crumbles bacon, almonds and thyme. Mix well. Place chicken breast between two pieces of plastic wrap. Working from center, pound chicken lightly to form a rectangle (about 1/8 thick). remove from plastic wrap. Repeat with other chicken breast. Sprinkle chicken with salt and pepper. Place half of filling mixture in center of each chicken breast. Roll chicken and secure with toothpick if necessary. Place rolls in microwaveable dish. Cook on high for 3-5 minutes or until chicken is done. (Turn plate once during cooking.)

Per serving: 2.2 g carbohydrates   241.4 calories
              0.9 g fiber   11.4 g fat
                                       31.4 g protein

Chicken with Garlic Butter
Serves 4

2	tablespoons	oil
4		chicken breast halves without skin -- cubed
12	ounces	fresh mushrooms -- sliced
1	tablespoon	minced garlic
1/2	teaspoon	salt
1/4	tablespoon	pepper
1	tablespoon	butter
1/4	cup	parsley -- chopped
1/4	cup	Swanson's® Fat-Free Chicken Broth

Heat oil in large skillet over medium heat. Add chicken cubes and mushrooms to oil. Stir constantly for about 3 minutes. Add garlic, salt and pepper. Continue stirring for another 3 minutes. Add butter, parsley and broth. Stir for another 1-2 minutes.

Per serving: 6.7 g carbohydrates   244.4 calories
               1.5 g fiber   11.6 g fat
                                           28.7 g protein

Coconut Shrimp
Serves 4

1	pound	shrimp -- peeled and deveined
1-1/2	cups	Kroger® unsweetened coconut -- flaked
1/2	cup	almond flour — see page 25
2	tablespoons	butter
2	tablespoons	oil
1		egg -- beaten
1	tablespoon	whipping cream

Wash and dry shrimp. In medium bowl, mix coconut and almond flour. In skillet, heat butter and oil over medium heat. In separate bowl, add whipping cream to beaten egg. Mix well. Coat shrimp with egg mixture and then coconut mixture. Fry in oil until golden, turning to cook evenly.

Per serving: 8.6 g carbohydrates   473.4 calories
              2.0 g fiber   37.3 g fat
                                         29.0 g protein

Crab Casserole
Serves 6

6-1/2	ounces	crab meat -- canned
8	ounces	cream cheese -- softened
1/4	cup	scallions -- chopped
4	cups	broccoli flowerets -- cooked
1	cup	cheddar cheese -- shredded
1	teaspoon	Spike® seasoning
1/3	cup	whipping cream
4	slices	bacon -- cooked and chopped
		salt -- to taste
		pepper -- to taste

In medium bowl, combine crab meat, cream cheese and scallions. In large greased baking dish, place 1/2 broccoli. Layer 1/2 crab mixture. Layer 1/2 of cheddar cheese and sprinkle with seasonings. Repeat layers. Pour whipping cream over layers. Top with chopped bacon.

Cover and bake at 350° for 20 minutes. Uncover and bake for an additional 15 minutes.

Per serving: 7.5 g carbohydrates   340.3 calories
              3.2 g fiber   27.2 g fat
                                          18.6 g protein

Crab Cakes
Serves 4

1/4	cup	Fearn® Soya Powder
1		egg
1	tablespoon	Worcestershire sauce
1	teaspoon	crab-boil seasoning
1	tablespoon	parsley
1	tablespoon	Hellman's® mayonnaise
1	pound	crab meat
2	tablespoons	oil

In large mixing bowl, combine soy powder, egg, Worcestershire sauce, seasonings and mayonnaise. Add crabmeat and mix. For into 4 patties. Heat oil in skillet before adding patties. Cook for 10 minutes per side or until crispy.

Per serving: 3.1 g carbohydrates 244.0 calories
1.0 g fiber 13.3 g fat
27.4 g protein

Creamy Chicken Packets
Serves 4

4		chicken breast halves without skin
4	tablespoons	butter
1	clove	garlic -- minced
1/2	cup	onion -- chopped
4	ounces	canned mushrooms -- drained
4	ounces	cream cheese -- cubed

Cut 4 sheets of aluminum foil 12 x 18". In center of each foil square, place a chicken breast topped with 1 TBSP. of butter. Add equal portions of garlic, onion and mushrooms. Place 1 ounce of cream cheese on each chicken breast. For each foil sheet, bring up foil side. Double fold top and ends to seal packet. Place packets on cookie sheet.

Bake at 350° for 45 minutes.

Per serving: 3.2 g carbohydrates 334.0 calories
1.0 g fiber 22.7 g fat
28.9 g protein

Fish Roll-Ups
Serves 6

2	pounds	fish fillets -- 6 pieces
		pepper -- to taste
6	tablespoons	Hellman's® mayonnaise
2	tablespoons	prepared mustard
1	teaspoon	lemon juice
1/4	teaspoon	thyme
1/2	pound	mushrooms -- chopped
1/4	cup	scallion -- chopped
6	tablespoons	butter
		paprika

Before starting, get six 12 x 12 squares of aluminum foil to make packets.

Place a fish fillet in the center of each foil square. Sprinkle with pepper. In separate bowl, combine mayonnaise, mustard, lemon juice and thyme. Place spoon of mixture on each fish fillet, dividing evenly. Repeat with mushrooms and scallions. Place 1 tablespoon of butter on each fillet. Sprinkle each with paprika. Fold each foil square toward the center and seal.

Bake at 325° for 25 minutes.

Per serving: 2.4 g carbohydrates   339.0 calories
               0.7 g fiber   23.8 g fat
                                           28.1 g protein

Meatloaf
Serves 6

2		eggs
1/2	cup	whipping cream
1/2	cup	Parmesan cheese
1/4	cup	onion -- finely chopped
1	teaspoon	Worcestershire sauce
1	teaspoon	Italian seasoning
2	pounds	ground beef
3	ounces	pork rinds -- crushed

Mix all ingredients well in a medium mixing bowl. Place in an ungreased 9x5 loaf pan.

Bake at 350° for 90 minutes or until done. Can be placed in 12 smaller pans and baked for 60 minutes or until done.

Per serving: 1.5 g carbohydrates   672.4 calories
              0.1 g fiber   56.0 g fat
                                           39.3 g protein

Pepper Steak Packets
Serves 4

1	pound	sirloin steak -- 1/2 inch thick
1/2	cup	green pepper -- sliced
1/2	cup	red pepper -- sliced
1/2	cup	onion -- chopped
1	can	Eden® black soybeans -- drained
1	cup	Pace® picante sauce
1	cup	cheddar cheese -- shredded

Cut steak lengthwise in half and then crosswise into 1/8" thick strips. Combine steak strips, peppers, onions, soy beans and picante sauce. Cut 4 sheets of aluminum foil 12 x 18". In center of each foil square, place one fourth of steak mixture. For each foil sheet, bring up foil side. Double fold top and ends to seal packet. Place packets on cookie sheet.

Bake at 450° for 20 minutes. Sprinkle with cheese before serving.

Per serving: 8.6 g carbohydrates   408.0 calories
              2.5 g fiber   27.2 g fat
                                       30.8 g protein

Portabello Mushroom Burgers
Serves 4

4		Portabello mushroom caps -- large
1/4	cup	balsamic vinegar
2	tablespoons	oil
1	teaspoon	dried basil
1	teaspoon	dried oregano
1	tablespoon	garlic -- minced
		salt -- to taste
		pepper -- to taste
4	slices	Provolone cheese

Cut stems off of mushrooms, and place smooth side up in a shallow dish. In a small bowl, whisk together the vinegar, oil, basil, oregano, garlic, and salt and pepper. Pour over mushrooms. Let stand at room temperature for around 15 minutes or so, turning twice. Reserve marinate.

Bake a 375° for 8 minutes on each side. Brush/baste with marinade frequently. Top with cheese during the last 2 minutes of baking.

Per serving: 5.6 g carbohydrates   473.9 calories
               0.2 g fiber   37.2 g fat
                                            30.0 g protein

Spicy Hamburgers
Serves 12

2	pounds	ground beef
1	pound	ground turkey
3		eggs
1	cup	Pace® picante sauce
2	cups	cheddar cheese -- shredded
		salt -- to taste
		pepper -- to taste

In large mixing bowl, mix all ingredients. Shape into 12 patties. Cook in skillet or on grill until done.

Per serving: 1.7 g carbohydrates   389.5 calories
              0.0 g fiber   30.5 g fat
                                         25.2 g protein

Seafood Casserole
Serves 4

1/2	pound	fresh mushrooms -- sliced
3	tablespoons	butter -- melted
1	teaspoon	salt
1/4	teaspoon	pepper
1	pound	crab meat -- lobster or shrimp
1	cup	sour cream
2	teaspoon	parsley -- chopped

Sauté mushrooms in melted butter for about 5 minutes. Add salt and pepper. Cool for 15 minutes. Add seafood, sour cream and parsley. Mix well. Place in baking dish.

Bake at 350° for 30 minutes.

Per serving: 5.4 g carbohydrates   326.7 calories
              0.8 g fiber   22.2 g fat
                                         26.5 g protein

Shrimp Creole
Serves 6

1	cup	onion -- chopped
1	cup	green pepper -- chopped
1/2	clove	garlic -- chopped
2	tablespoons	butter
2	cups	Italian tomatoes -- chopped
1/2	teaspoon	paprika
		salt -- to taste
		pepper -- to taste
1/2	pound	shrimp -- cooked

Sauté onions, green peppers and garlic in butter. Simmer until tender. Add tomatoes and seasonings. Boil for 5 minutes. Add shrimp. Boil for another 10 minutes.

Per serving: 5.0 g carbohydrates   94.7 calories
              1.2 g fiber   4.7 g fat
                                     8.6 g protein

Shrimp and Artichokes
Serves 8

2	tablespoons	butter
14	ounces	artichoke hearts -- drained and chopped
2	pounds	shrimp -- cooked and peeled
1/2	pound	fresh mushrooms -- sliced
4-1/2	tablespoons	butter
4-1/2	tablespoons	Fearn® Soya Powder
1	cup	whipping cream
1/2	cup	half & half
		salt -- to taste
		pepper -- to taste
1/4	cup	water
1	tablespoon	Worcestershire sauce
1/4	cup	Parmesan cheese -- shredded

Spread drained artichokes in greased casserole dish. Layer shrimp on top. Melt remaining butter in skillet. Add mushrooms and cook for 4-5 minutes. Pour over shrimp. Melt 4-1/2 tablespoons butter in pan. Stir in soya powder. Add whipping cream and half & half. Stir over medium heat until thickened. Add salt and pepper. Add water and Worcestershire sauce and mix well. Pour over shrimp. Sprinkle cheese on top of casserole.

Bake at 375° for 20 minutes.

Per serving: 10.8 g carbohydrates   382.7 calories
              3.5 g fiber   25.5 g fat
                                       29.0 g protein

Shrimp Foo Young
Serves 4

8		eggs
2	tablespoons	water
1	teaspoon	soy sauce
1/2	teaspoon	salt
1/8	teaspoon	pepper
1	cup	shrimp, cooked -- small
1/2	cup	green pepper -- chopped
1/2	cup	scallions -- sliced
1/2	cup	bean sprouts
2	tablespoons	butter

In medium bowl, combine eggs, water, soy sauce, salt and pepper. Mix well. Stir in shrimp, green pepper, scallions and bean sprouts. Melt butter in large skillet. Pour in egg mixture. When bottom of egg mixture begins to set, lift edge to let uncooked mixture to move to skillet. Continue cooking until eggs are done. Fold in half before serving.

Per serving: 3.5 g carbohydrates   246.7 calories
              0.8 g fiber   14.9 g fat
                                       23.8 g protein

Stuffed Peppers
Serves 6

3		bell peppers -- red, green, yellow
1	pound	ground beef
1	teaspoon	onion powder
1	cup	cauliflower -- shredded
6	tablespoons	tomato paste
6	tablespoons	cheddar cheese -- shredded

Cut peppers in half and blanche. Place in 9x13 baking dish. Cook ground beef and onion powder in skillet. Do not drain, add cauliflower. Cook until cauliflower is tender. Place cooked mixture in pepper shells.

Bake at 350° for 45 minutes.

Place 1 tablespoon of tomato paste and cheddar cheese on each pepper. Bake for an additional 15 minutes or until cheese has melted.

Per serving: 5.8 g carbohydrates   287.9 calories
              1.4 g fiber   22.7 g fat
                                      15.4 g protein

Stuffed Portabella Mushrooms
Serves 4

4	ounces	sausage
4		Portabella mushroom caps
1-1/2	teaspoons	dried thyme
1-1/2	teaspoons	garlic — crushed
		salt — to taste
		pepper — to taste
10	ounces	frozen chopped spinach – cooked and drained
4	ounces	Brie cheese — rind removed

Cook sausage, drain, crumble and set aside. In small bowl, add garlic, thyme, salt and pepper to cooked spinach. Mix well. Place mushrooms in baking dish. evenly fill caps with spinach mixture. Layer with sausage. Top with Brie.

Bake at 350° for 12-15 minutes. Broil for 2 minutes until cheese is browned.

Per serving: 5.1 g carbohydrates   240.8 calories
              2.3 g fiber   19.6 g fat
                                     12.2 g protein

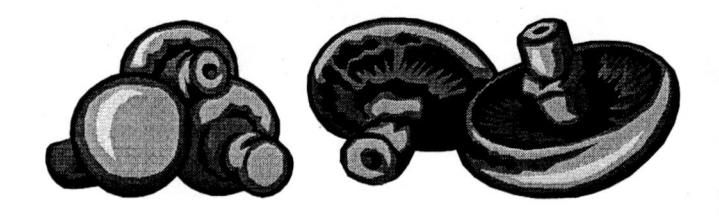

ENTREES

Taco Bake
Serves 4

1/2	pound	ground beef
1/2	pound	ground turkey
15	ounces	Eden® black soybeans -- rinsed and drained
4	ounces	green chili peppers -- rinsed and drained
1	package	taco seasoning mix
1	cup	sour cream
1	cup	cheddar cheese -- shredded

Cook ground beef and ground turkey in skillet over medium heat. Break into small pieces. Cook until no longer pink. Stir in beans, peppers and seasoning. Spread mixture into 9x9 baking dish. Spread sour cream layer over meats. Sprinkle cheese over top.

Bake at 350° for 30 minutes.

Per serving: 12.1 g carbohydrates   608.0 calories
              6.0 g fiber   46.2 g fat
                                       37.6 g protein

Taco Meat
Serves 4

1	pound	ground beef
3/4	cup	water
1/2	cup	onion -- chopped
2	tablespoons	chili powder
1	teaspoon	salt
1/2	teaspoon	ground cumin
1	clove	garlic -- crushed

In medium skillet, cook ground beef until done. Drain. Stir in water, onion, seasonings and garlic. Heat to boiling then reduce heat. Simmer uncovered, stirring, until thickened - about 10 minutes. Serve in Cheese Taco Shells (see page 46).

Per serving: 3.2 g carbohydrates   369.3 calories
              1.6 g fiber   30.9 g fat
                                       19.6 g protein

Favorite Recipes

Almond Brownies
Serves 16

1/4	cup	butter -- softened
1	ounce	unsweetened baking chocolate squares -- melted
2	tablespoons	water
1	cup	almond flour -- see page 25
3/4	cup	sugar substitute — see page 21
1	teaspoon	not/Sugar®
1	teaspoon	vanilla extract
1/4	cup	Fearn® Soya Powder
1	teaspoon	xanthan gum
2		eggs
1/2	cup	walnuts -- chopped

In medium mixing bowl, combine butter, chocolate, water, almond flour, sugar substitute, not/Sugar®, vanilla, soya powder, xanthan gum and eggs. Mix well. Fold in walnuts. Spread in well greased 8x8 baking pan.

Bake at 325° for 20 minutes. Cool before cutting.

Per serving: 4.2 g carbohydrates   96.4 calories
                0.8 fiber   8.4 g fat
                                             3.0 g protein

Almond Cookies
Serves 24

1-1/4	cups	almond Flour -- see page 25
1	cup	sugar substitute — see page 21
1		egg
1/2	teaspoon	almond extract
1/4	cup	butter -- softened
1	teaspoon	not/Sugar®

Mix all ingredients well in medium bowl. Form into 24 balls. Place on sprayed cookie sheet. Gently flatten cookie balls.

Bake at 350° for 8 minutes.

Per serving: 2.5 g carbohydrates   54.7 calories
0.1 g fiber   4.8 g fat
1.3 g protein

Almond Meringue Cookies
Serves 24

2		egg whites
1/8	teaspoon	cream of tartar
1/2	cup	sugar substitute — see page 21
1/2	cup	almond flour -- see page 25

Preheat oven to 325°.

In large bowl, whip egg whites until frothy. Add cream of tarter and beat until stiff peaks form. In separate bowl, combine sugar substitute and almond flour. Fold into egg whites. Mix well. Spoon mixture (24 mounds) onto cookie sheet lined with parchment paper.

Bake at reduced heat of 250° for 1 hour.

Per serving: 1.1 g carbohydrates   15.8 calories
0.0 g fiber   1.1 g fat
0.7 g protein

DESSERTS

Almond Pie Crust
Serves 12

1-1/4	cups	almond flour -- see page 25
2	tablespoons	sugar substitute — see page 21
1/8	teaspoon	salt
2	tablespoons	butter -- melted
2	tablespoons	oat flour

In a medium mixing bowl, combine all ingredients and mix well. Chill for 30 minutes. Press mixture into an 8 inch pie plate.

Bake at 375° for 10-12 minutes.

Per serving: 3.6 g carbohydrates   83.2 calories
               0.1 g fiber   7.3 g fat
                                            2.2 g protein

Variations: Substitute pecan flour, brazil nut flour, hazelnut flour or walnut flour for the almond flour.

Plain Pie Crust
Serves 12

1		egg
1/4	teaspoon	salt
1	cup	oat flour — see page 25
3	tablespoons	butter — melted

In a medium mixing bowl, combine egg, salt, oat flour and butter. Mix well. Dough will be sticky. Chill for 30 minutes. Roll out dough between 2 sheets of waxed paper. Place dough in 8 in pie plate.

Bake at 425° for 18 minutes. (Place second pie pan on top of uncooked dough to retain shape while cooking.)

Per serving: 5.1 g carbohydrates   60.7 calories
               1.0 g fiber   3.7 g fat
                                            1.7 g protein

DESSERTS
132

Almond Pound Cake (Cupcakes)
Serves 12

1/2	cup	butter
4	ounces	cream cheese -- softened
5		eggs
2	cups	almond flour -- see page 25
1	cup	sugar substitute — see page 21
1	teaspoon	not/Sugar®
1	teaspoon	baking powder
1	teaspoon	lemon extract
1	teaspoon	vanilla extract

Cream butter and cream cheese together. Add eggs and mix after each one. In separate bowl, combine almond flour, sugar substitute, not/Sugar® and baking powder. Add dry mixture to egg mixture a little at a time. Mix well. Add flavorings and stir. Pour into well greased 9" cake pan.

Bake at 350° for 50-55 minutes.

Per serving: 7.1 g carbohydrates   234.4 calories
               0.1 g fiber   21.3 g fat
                                          6.3 g protein

Variation: For cupcakes, our into 12 paper lined cupcake tins. Bake at 325° for 25-30 minutes.

Black and White Brownies
Serves 36

1	cup	butter
4	ounces	unsweetened baking chocolate squares
2	cups	sugar substitute — see page 21
1	tablespoon	not/Sugar®
3		eggs
1	cup	Fearn® Soya Powder
1/2	teaspoon	salt
1	teaspoon	vanilla extract
1	cup	pecans -- finely chopped
1	teaspoon	xanthan gum
8	ounces	cream cheese -- softened
1/2	cup	sugar substitute — see page 21
1	teaspoon	not/Sugar®
1		egg
1	teaspoon	vanilla extract

First layer: Melt butter over low heat or in microwave. Remove from heat and add sugar substitute, not/Sugar® and eggs. Mix well. Add soya powder, salt, vanilla, pecans and xanthan gum. Mix well again. Spread in a greased 9x13 baking pan.

In separate bowl, combine cream cheese, sugar substitute, not/Sugar®, egg and vanilla. Beat at medium spread for 2-3 minutes. Spread cream cheese mixture over first layer and make swirls with a toothpick.

Bake at 350° for 40 minutes. Cool before cutting. Chill overnight before serving if possible.

Per serving: 4.1 g carbohydrates   119.3 calories
               1.2 g fiber   11.1 g fat
                                           2.7 g protein

Black Bean Brownies
Serves 24

4	ounces	unsweetened chocolate
1/2	pound	butter
1	cup	Eden® black soybeans -- drained and rinsed
4		eggs
2	cups	sugar substitute — see page 21
1	tablespoon	not/Sugar®
1	teaspoon	vanilla extract
1	cup	walnuts -- chopped

In a small saucepan, melt the chocolate with the butter. Set aside to cool. Place black soybeans in blender or food processor. Blend until pureed. (Use a small amount at a time if necessary.) With mixer, beat eggs together with sugar substitute. Add the melted chocolate mixture, vanilla and not/Sugar®. Mix well. Add bean puree and again mix well. Fold in chopped walnuts. Pour into a 9x13" baking pan.

Bake at 350° for 45-50 minutes.

Per serving: 5.2 carbohydrates   153.9 calories
              1.7 g fiber   14.6 g fat
                                         3.1 g protein

Chess Pie
Serves 12

1-1/2	cups	suagr substitute — see page 21
1/2	cup	butter -- melted
4	teaspoons	almond flour -- see page 25
1	tablespoon	white vinegar
1	teaspoon	vanilla extract
3		eggs -- beaten
1	tablespoon	not/Sugar®
1		almond pie crust — see page 131

In medium bowl, combine sugar substitute, butter, almond flour, white vinegar, vanilla and not/Sugar®. Add beaten eggs and mix well. Pour into prepared almond pie crust.

Bake at 350° for 50 minutes. Let cool before cutting.

Per serving: 6.7 g carbohydrates   196.7 calories
              0.3 g fiber   18.2 g fat
                                       3.7 g protein

Chocolate Almond Sponge Cake
Serves 8

5		eggs -- separated
3/4	cup	sugar substitute — see page 21
1	teaspoon	not/Sugar®
2	tablespoons	unsweetened cocoa powder
1/2	teaspoon	vanilla extract
1/4	teaspoon	ReaLemon® lemon juice
1-2/3	cups	almond flour -- see page 25

In small bowl, beat egg yolks with sugar substitute and not/Sugar®. Stir in cocoa and vanilla. In separate bowl, beat egg whites with lemon juice until firm. Fold almond flour and yolk mixture into egg whites. Pour batter into greased 9" cake pan (spring form is best).

Bake at 350° for 25-30 minutes. Remove cake from pan and let cool. Sprinkle with sugar substitute before serving.

Per serving: 9.0 g carbohydrates   175.9 calories
              0.6 g fiber   13.6 g fat
                                       7.7 g protein

Variation: Cut the cake horizontally into 2 layers. Spread Chocolate Filling with walnuts (see page 138) between the layers.

Chocolate Meringue Torte
Serves 16

2/3	cup	pecans -- finely chopped
3		egg whites
1/2	teaspoon	almond extract
1/4	teaspoon	salt
3/4	cup	sugar substitute — see page 21
1	teaspoon	not/Sugar®
1		chocolate filling — see page 138

Place pecans in blender, food processor or coffee grinder. (Use only small amounts at a time.) Grind until flour or meal consistency. In separate bowl, beat egg whites with almond extract until frothy. Gradually add sugar substitute, not/Sugar® and salt. Fold in nuts. Using an 8 inch cake pan, cut 4 circles from parchment paper and place on two cookie sheets. Spread meringue on each parchment paper circle.

Bake at 300° for 35 minutes. Cool before carefully removing paper.

Spread chocolate filling on two layers of meringue. Place second layer on top and spread remaining filling around sides. Chill overnight before cutting.

Per serving: 5.6 g carbohydrates   165.4 calories
              0.9 g fiber   15.5 g fat
                                       2.6 g protein

Chocolate Filling
Serves 16

8	ounces	cream cheese -- softened
1	tablespoon	half & half
1-1/4	cups	sugar substitute — see page 21
2	teaspoons	not/Sugar®
2	ounces	unsweetened baking chocolate squares
2	tablespoons	butter
1	cup	whipping cream -- whipped
1	teaspoon	vanilla extract

Blend cream cheese with half & half. Add sugar substitute and not/Sugar®. Mix well. Melt chocolate and butter in pan or microwave. Add cheese mixture, whipped cream and vanilla to chocolate. Spread filling on two layers of meringue. Place second layer on top and spread remaining filling around sides. Chill overnight before cutting.

Per serving: 3.9 g carbohydrates   141.4 calories
              0.7 g fiber   13.9 g fat
                                     1.8 g protein

Chocolate Peanut Butter Bits
Serves 12

1	ounce	unsweetened baking chocolate
1/3	cup	Fifty-50® Peanut Butter
2	tablespoons	butter
1/3	cup	Frigo® ricotta, part skim
1/2	cup	sugar substitute — see page 21

Combine chocolate, peanut butter and butter in small glass dish. Microwave just until melted. Stir until well mixed. Add ricotta cheese and sugar substitute and mix until smooth. Drop 12 spoonfuls onto waxed paper. Chill until firm.

Per serving: 3.2 g carbohydrates   90.8 calories
              0.8 g fiber   7.8 g fat
                                     3.3 g protein

Coconut Almond Cake
Serves 8

6		eggs -- separated
2/3	cup	sugar substitute — see page 21
1	teaspoon	not/Sugar®
1/4	teaspoon	ReaLemon® lemon juice
2	cups	almond flour -- see page 25
1	cup	Kroger® unsweetened coconut -- ground

In small bowl, beat egg yolks with sugar substitute and not/Sugar®. In separate bowl, whip egg whites with lemon juice until firm. Fold almond flour, ground coconut and yolk mixture into egg whites. Pour batter into greased 9" cake pan (spring form is best).

Bake at 350° for 25-30 minutes. Remove cake from pan and let cool. Sprinkle with sugar substitute before serving.

Per serving: 10.5 g carbohydrates   250.8 calories
              0.8 g fiber   20.8 g fat
                                        9.6 g protein

Variation: Cut the cake horizontally into 2 layers. Spread Whipped Cream Filling (see page 151) between the layers.

"Graham Cracker" Crust
Serves 12

9		Bran-a-crisp® crackers
1/3	cup	butter -- melted
4	packets	sugar substitute — see page 21
1/2	teaspoon	cinnamon

Place crackers in blender, food processor or coffee grinder. (Use 1 or 2 at a time.) Grind until flour or meal consistency. Place flour in a medium bowl and add sugar substitute, cinnamon and melted butter. Mix with hands. Press into an 8" pie tin.

Bake at 300° for about 10 minutes.

Per serving: 2.8 g carbohydrates 60.1 calories
2.4 g fiber 5.1 g fat
0.9 g protein

# Fudge Macaroon Pie
Serves 12

3	ounces	unsweetened baking chocolate squares
1/2	cup	butter
3		eggs -- beaten
3/4	cup	sugar substitute — see page 21
1/2	cup	Fearn® Soya Powder
1	teaspoon	vanilla extract
2	teaspoons	not/Sugar®
2-2/3	cups	Kroger® unsweetened coconut -- flaked
2/3	cup	sweetened condensed milk substitute -- see page 131

Melt chocolate and butter in saucepan over low heat or in microwave. Stir in eggs, sugar substitute, soya powder, vanilla and not/Sugar.® Spread in 9 inch pie plate pushing up slightly on sides.

In separate bowl, combine coconut and condensed milk substitute. Spoon mixture over chocolate crust, leaving a 1/2 - 1 inch border.

Bake at 350° for 30 minutes. Cool before cutting.

Per serving: 8.0 g carbohydrates   255.1 calories
              3.2 g fiber   24.5 g fat
                                         5.3 g protein

DESSERTS

Ice Cream - Hand Cranked
Serves 16

2	cups	whipping cream
2	cups	half & half
1	cup	sugar substitute — see page 21
1-1/4	cups	walnuts -- chopped
1-1/2	teaspoons	vanilla extract
1/2	teaspoon	cinnamon
1/4	teaspoon	salt
4	tablespoons	not/Sugar®

Combine all ingredients in ice churn container. Follow freezer directions.

Per serving: 5.8 g carbohydrates   211.4 calories
              1.4 g fiber   20.0 g fat
                                      3.9 g protein

Variations: Experiment with different combinations of flavorings, nuts, zero carb chocolate chips.

Icing
Serves 12

8	ounces	cream cheese -- softened
2-1/2	tablespoons	butter -- softened
4	packets	sugar substitute — see page 21
1/2	teaspoon	vanilla extract

In small mixing bowl, blend cream cheese with butter. Add sugar substitute and vanilla. Mix well.

Per serving: 0.9 g carbohydrates   88.4 calories
              0.0 g fiber   9.0 g fat
                                      1.5g protein

DESSERTS
143

Jell-o® Substitute
Serves 4

1/2	package	unsweetened drink mix -- any flavor
1	package	Knox® unflavored gelatin
1/2	cup	sugar substitute - see page 21
2	cups	water

Heat 1 cup of water to boiling in microwave. Add gelatin and stir to dissolve. Add remaining water, drink mix and sugar substitute. Pour into desired container. Chill to set before serving.

Per serving: 3.0 g carbohydrates   37.0 calories
              0.0 g fiber   0.0 g fat
                                       6.0 g protein

Variation: Substitute 2 cups of any diet drink (carbonated or non-carbonated) for the unsweetened drink mix, sugar substitute and water.

Key Lime Pie
Serves 12

2/3	cup	water
1	package	sugar-free gelatin mix -- small, lime flavor
1/3	cup	whipping cream
16	ounces	cream cheese -- softened
2	packets	sugar substitute -- see page 21
1		almond pie crust -- see page 131

Heat water to boiling in microwave. Add gelatin and stir until dissolved. Set aside to cool. In medium bowl, whip whipping cream until stiff. In separate bowl, whip cream cheese and sugar substitute until smooth. Slowly add gelatin mixture to cream cheese. Mix well. Add whipped cream and mix slowly. Spoon to almond crust. Chill to set before serving.

Per serving: 4.7 g carbohydrates   254.8 calories
              0.0 g fiber   24.8 g fat
                                       5.4 g protein

DESSERTS

Lemon Meringue Pie
Serves 12

1	package	sugar-free pudding mix -- small, lemon flavor
2/3	cup	sugar substitute — see page 21
2-1/4	cups	water
3		egg yolks
2	tablespoons	lemon juice
2	tablespoons	butter
4	ounces	cream cheese -- softened
2	teaspoons	not/Sugar®
2	drops	yellow food coloring -- optional
3		egg whites
1/4	teaspoon	cream of tartar
6	tablespoons	sugar substitute — see page 21
1/2	teaspoon	vanilla extract
1		almond pie crust -- see page 131

Combine pudding mix, sugar substitute and water in medium saucepan. Mix with wire whisk until smooth. Cook over medium heat, stirring constantly, just until boiling. Be careful not to scorch bottom of mixture. Remove from heat. Stir in lemon juice, butter, cream cheese, not /Sugar® and food coloring until well mixed. Let stand for 5 minutes before pouring into almond pie crust.

Beat egg whites and cream of tarter until foamy. Beat in sugar substitute, 1 tablespoon at a time. Continue beating until stiff and glossy. Blend in vanilla. Spoon over pie filling.

Bake at 425° for 8-10 minutes until meringue is slightly browned. Cool before cutting.

Per serving:	8.0 g carbohydrates	183.3 calories
	0.2 g fiber	15.6 g fat
		4.4 g protein

DESSERTS

Pumpkin Pie
Serves 12

2		eggs
16	ounces	canned pumpkin
3/4	cup	sugar substitute — see page 21
1/2	teaspoon	salt
1	teaspoon	ground cinnamon
1/2	teaspoon	ginger
1/2	teaspoon	ground cloves
1-2/3	cups	half & half
1		almond pie crust -- see page 131

In medium bowl, slightly beat eggs. Add pumpkin, sugar substitute and all spices. Mix well. Pour mixture into almond pie crust.

Bake at 425° for 15 minutes. Reduce oven temperature to 350°. Bake for an additional 45 minutes, or until knife inserted in center comes out clean. Let cool before cutting.

Per serving: 9.4 g carbohydrates   170.4 calories
              1.2 g fiber   13.9 g fat
                                     4.4 g protein

Quick Treat
Serves 8

16	ounces	cream cheese -- softened
1	cup	whipping cream
1	teaspoon	unsweetened drink mix -- any flavor
1/4	cup	sugar substitute — see page 21

Whip cream cheese in mixer. Add whipping cream, drink mix and sugar substitute and blend until smooth. Store in refrigerator.

Per serving: 3.1 g carbohydrates   303.5 calories
              0.0 g fiber   30.8 g fat
                                     4.9 g protein

DESSERTS

Sugar Cookies
Serves 24

1-1/4	cups	almond flour -- See page 25
1	cup	sugar substitute — see page 21
1	teaspoon	not/Sugar®
1		egg
1/2	teaspoon	butter extract
1	teaspoon	vanilla extract
1/4	cup	butter -- softened

In medium mixing bowl, combine almond flour and sugar substitute. Add not/Sugar®, egg, extracts and butter. Blend well. Form into 24 balls. Place on sprayed cookie sheet. Gently flatten cookie balls.

Bake at 350° for 8 minutes.

Per serving: 2.5 g carbohydrates   54.7 calories
               0.1 g fiber   4.8 g fat
                                          1.3 g protein

Chocolate Meringue Cookies
Serves 16

3		egg whites
1/8	teaspoon	cream of tartar
1/3	cup	sugar substitute — see page 21
2	tablespoons	unsweetened cocoa powder
1/4	cup	pecan meal -- see page 25

In large bowl, whip egg whites until frothy. Add cream of tarter and beat until stiff peaks form. In separate bowl, combine sugar substitute and cocoa. Fold into white whites. Separately, fold in pecans. Mix well. Spoon mixture (16 mounds) onto cookie sheet lined with parchment paper.

Bake at 250° for 60 minutes. Let cool before removing from cookie sheet.

Per serving: 1.1 g carbohydrates   12.7 calories
               0.3 g fiber   0.7 g fat
                                          0.9 g protein

Sweetened Condensed Milk Substitute
Serves 1

1	cup	whipping cream
2		egg yolks
1/3	cup	sugar substitute — see page 21
1	tablespoon	not/Sugar®

Combine all ingredients in small saucepan. Cook over low heat until thickened, stirring constantly. This is will replace one can.

Per serving: 18.6 g carbohydrates   985.4 calories
              3.4 g fiber   98.3 g fat
                                       10.5 g protein

Tofu Pie
Serves 8

1	package	sugar-free gelatin mix -- small, any flavor
1	cup	hot water
1/2	cup	cold water
8	ounces	tofu -- drained
1	tablespoon	lemon juice
1		"graham cracker" crust — see page 140

Dissolve gelatin in boiling water, stirring until completely dissolved. Add cold water and set aside to cool. Place tofu in blender. Add lemon juice and blend until smooth (about 1 minute). Add cooled gelatin to blender and whip until smooth. (Mixture will be thin.) Pour into "Graham Cracker" crust. Chill until firm. Garnish with whipped cream, if desired.

Per serving: 3.7 g carbohydrates   93.3 calories
              0.4 g fiber   9.1 g fat
                                      0.4 g protein

DESSERTS

Valentine Pie
Serves 12

1/2	cup	Kroger® unsweetened coconut -- shredded
5	tablespoons	unsweetened cocoa powder
1-1/2	cups	sugar substitute — see page 21
2	teaspoons	not/Sugar®
1/4	cup	butter -- softened
2		eggs
1/2	cup	half & half
3/4	cup	pecan halves
1		almond pie crust -- see page 131

In mixing bowl, combine coconut, cocoa, sugar substitute and not/Sugar®. Add butter, eggs and half & half. Mix well. Fold in pecan halves. Pour into prepared almond pie crust.

Bake at 400° for 30 minutes. Cool before cutting.

Per serving: 9.0 g carbohydrates   210.5 calories
              1.4 g fiber   19.1 g fat
                                           4.3 g protein

Icing – 2
Serves 16

8	ounces	cream cheese
3	tablespoons	sugar substitute – see page 21
1	cup	half & half

In mixing bowl, mix all ingredients until smooth. Adjust amount of half & half until desired consistency.

Per serving: 1.3 g carbohydrates   70.3 calories
              0.0 g fiber   6.7 g fat
                                           1.5 g protein

DESSERTS
149

Walnut Cake
Serves 8

6		eggs -- separated
3/4	cup	sugar substitute — see page 21
1	teaspoon	not/Sugar®
1/4	teaspoon	ReaLemon® lemon juice
1-2/3	cups	ground walnuts -- see page 25

In small bowl, beat egg yolks with sugar substitute and not/Sugar®. In separate bowl, whip egg whites with lemon juice until firm. Fold ground nuts and yolk mixture into egg whites. Pour batter into greased 9" cake pan (spring form is best).

Bake at 350° for 35-40 minutes. Remove cake from pan and let cool. Sprinkle with Splenda before serving.

Per serving: 5.1 g carbohydrates   166.1 calories
               1.3 g fiber   14.1 g fat
                                          6.5 g protein

Variation: Cut the cake horizontally into 2 layers. Spread Whipped Cream Filling with walnuts (see page 151) between the layers.

Walnut Macaroon Cookies
Serves 36

2	cups	walnuts
3		egg whites
3	tablespoons	Kroger® unsweetened coconut -- flaked
1/2	teaspoon	coconut extract
1/2	cup	sugar substitute — see page 21

Place walnuts in blender, food processor or coffee grinder. (Use only small amounts at a time.) Grind until flour or meal consistency. Add coconut flakes to last batch of walnuts and blend well.

In a separate bowl, whip egg whites until fluffy peaks form. Add coconut extract and sugar substitute. Mix well. Fold nut flour mixture into egg white mixture. Mix well. Spoon 36 small mounds onto sprayed cookie sheet.

Bake at 350° for 15 minutes.

Per serving: 1.6 g carbohydrates   47.5 calories
              0.4 g fiber   4.3 g fat
                                     1.3 g protein

Whipped Cream Filling
Serves 12

1-1/2	teaspoons	Knox® unflavored gelatin
2	tablespoons	cold water
1/2	cup	half & half
2		egg yolks — slightly beaten
3/4	cup	sugar substitute — see page 21
1/2	cup	whipping cream — whipped
1	teaspoon	almond extract
1/2	teaspoon	vanilla extract
1/2	cup	almond slivers — toasted

In a small bowl, sprinkle gelatin in water. In a small saucepan, heat the half & half until it begins to simmer. In a separate bowl, combine the egg yolks and sugar substitute. Gradually add the egg mixture to the hot half & half, stirring until thick. Add gelatin mixture and cook over low heat, stirring constantly, until dissolved. Remove from heat. Let cool. Fold in whipped cream, flavorings and almonds. Chill until thick enough to spread.

Per serving: 3.4 g carbohydrates   108.1 calories
              0.4 g fiber   8.9 g fat
                                       4.3 g protein

Variation: Substitute other nuts for the almond slivers.

Cream Cheese bars
Serves 16

5	tablespoons	butter
1/3	cup	sugar substitute — see page 21
1	cup	Fearn® Soya Powder
1/2	teaspoon	not/Sugar®
1	teaspoon	xanthan Gum
1/2	cup	walnuts -- finely chopped — see page 25
8	ounces	cream cheese -- softened
1/2	cup	sugar substitute — see page 21
1		egg
2	tablespoons	whipping cream
1	tablespoon	lemon juice
1/2	teaspoon	vanilla extract
1	teaspoon	not/Sugar®

Crust: Cream together butter and sugar substitute. Add soya powder, not/Sugar®, xanthan gum and walnuts. Reserve 1/2 of mixture. Spread rest of nut mixture in greased 8x8 baking pan. Press lightly.

Bake at 350° for 10 minutes.

Filling: Combine cream cheese, sugar substitute, egg, whipping cream, lemon juice, vanilla and not/Sugar®. Mix well. Pour filling over baked crust. Spread reserved nut mixture over cream cheese layer.

Bake at 350° for 25 minutes. Chill before cutting.

Per serving: 4.3 g carbohydrates   145.9 calories
              1.4 g fiber   12.9 g fat
                                         4.9 g protein

INDEX OF RECIPES

APPETIZERS & SNACKS
    Black Bean Dip 29
    Cheese Crackers. 29
    Cheese Spread 30
    Cinnamon Crunchies 30
    Crab & Spinach Spread 31
    Dried Beef Roll-ups 31
    Horseradish Mold 32
    Meatball Bites 33
    Pepperoni Bites 32
    Popsicles 33
    Scallion Bean Pancakes 34
    Shrimp Dip 35
    Spinach-Garlic Spread 35

BREADS
    Basic Bread 45
    Cheese Bread 46
    Cheese Taco Shells 46
    Cinnamon Nut Bread 47
    Cinnamon Rolls 48
    Crepes 46
    Herb and Cheese Muffins 51
    Herbed Crackers 49
    Wheat Germ - Cheese Bars 50

BREAKFAST DISHES
    Chili-Cheese Oven Omelet 71
    Cottage Cheese Pancakes 67
    Cream of "Wheat" 65
    "French Toast" Eggs 65
    Granola 66
    Ham and Cheese Roll 68
    Ham and Egg "Cupcakes" 67
    Pancakes 69
    Sausage Spinach Bake 70
    Strawberry Jam 66

DRINKS

Café au Lait 39
Café Latte 39
Cappuccino 40
Frappuccino (Frozen) 40
Hot Chocolate 41
Lemonade 41
Mochaccino 42

DESSERTS

Almond Brownies 129
Almond Cookies 130
Almond Meringue Cookies 130
Almond Pie Crust 131
Almond Pound Cake (Cupcakes) 132
Black and White Brownies 133
Black Bean Brownies 134
Chess Pie 135
Chocolate Almond Sponge Cake 136
Chocolate Filling 138
Chocolate Meringue Cookies 146
Chocolate Meringue Torte 137
Chocolate Peanut Butter Bits 138
Coconut Almond Cake 139
Cream Cheese Bars 152
Fudge Macaroon Pie 141
"Graham Cracker" Crust 140
Ice Cream - Hand Cranked 142
Icing 142
Icing 2 148
Jell-o® Substitute 143
Key Lime Pie 143
Lemon Meringue Pie 144
Plain Pie Crust 131
Pumpkin Pie 145
Quick Treat 145
Sugar Cookies 146
Sweetened Condensed Milk Substitute 147
Tofu Pie 147
Valentine Pie 148
Walnut Cake 149
Walnut Macaroon Cookies 150
Whipped Cream Filling 151

ENTREES

Almond Chicken 101
Baked Cheesy Pork Chops 102
Beef Stroganoff 103
Cabbage "Noodles" 102
Cabbage Rolls 104
Cheesy Broiled Flounder 105
Chicken Cacciatore 106
Chicken Dijon 105
Chicken Excelsior 107
Chicken Fried "Rice" 108
Chicken Kiev 109
Chicken Rolls Almondine 110
Chicken with Garlic Butter 111
Coconut Shrimp 112
Crab Casserole 113
Crab Cakes 114
Creamy Chicken Packets 114
Fish Roll-Ups 115
Fried Chicken 106
Meatloaf 116
Parmesan Chicken 101
Pepper Steak Packets 117
Portabello Mushroom Burgers 118
Seafood Casserole 119
Shrimp and Artichokes 121
Shrimp Creole 120
Shrimp Foo Young 122
Spicy Hamburgers 119
Stuffed Peppers 123
Stuffed Portabella Mushrooms 124
Taco Bake 125
Taco Meat 125

SALADS

Coleslaw 75
Bacon - Cauliflower Toss 78
Florentine Salad 79
Fresh Mushroom Salad 80
Green Bean Salad 81
Mushroom - Spinach Toss 80
Pickled Beets 75
Sauerkraut Slaw 77
Spinach Salad 76
Wilted Lettuce Salad 77

SAUCES

Caesar Dressing 56
Cheese Sauce 59
Hollandaise sauce 60

SOUPS

Bean and Sausage Soup 55
Cauliflower Soup 57
Cheeseburger Soup 59
Cheese Soup 58
Cheese "Potato" Soup 58
Chili with Beans 56
Clam Chowder 60
Tuscan Bean Soup with Sausage 61

VEGETABLES

Asparagus Casserole 85
Baked Beans 86
Broccoli with Pecans 86
"French Fries" 87
Fried Eggplant 97
Fried Spinach 87
Green Beans with Dill Sauce 88
Mexican Spinach with Beans 89
Mushroom Casserole 90
Posh Squash 91
"Potato" Casserole 92
Refried Beans 89
Roasted Cauliflower with Coriander 97
Spinach Soufflé 93
Spinach Squares 94
Zucchini Parmesan 95
Zucchini Patties 96

More! "Low Carb Recipes Fast & Easy" (and Original Book)

Order Form

QTY	PRICE	KY ONLY TAX	SHIPPING (1-2 books)	Book 1 or 2?	TOTAL
____	$15.95	6%	$2.50 (10-15 day delivery)	_____	_____
____	$15.95	6%	$4.50 (2-3 day delivery)	_____	_____

____ Enclosed is my check/money order for $_____

____ Please charge to my   ☐ VISA or   ☐ Master Card

Card No._____ Exp. Date_____

Name on card _____

Signature _____

Please send cookbook(s) to:

Name _____

Address _____

City _____ State _____ Zip _____

Telephone _____

Please return form to:

Brass Pig, LLC
PO Box 43091
Louisville, KY 40253

1-888-229-9677
Fax 1-502-228-7345

www.LowCarbRecipes.com